SCIENTIFIC AMERICAN EXPLORES BIG IDEAS

The Debate over Creationism vs. Evolution

The Editors of *Scientific American*

SCIENTIFIC AMERICAN EDUCATIONAL PUBLISHING

New York

Published in 2024 by Scientific American Educational Publishing
in association with **The Rosen Publishing Group**
2544 Clinton Street, Buffalo NY 14224

Contains material from Scientific American®, a division of Springer Nature America, Inc., reprinted by permission, as well as original material from The Rosen Publishing Group®.

First Edition

Scientific American
Lisa Pallatroni: Project Editor

Rosen Publishing
David Kuchta: Compiling Editor
Michael Moy: Senior Graphic Designer

Cataloging-in-Publication Data
Names: Scientific American, Inc.
Title: The debate over creationism vs. evolution / edited by the Scientific American Editors.
Description: New York : Scientific American Educational Publishing, 2024. |
Series: Scientific American explores big ideas | Includes glossary and index.
Identifiers: ISBN 9781725349421 (pbk.) | ISBN 9781725349438
(library bound)| ISBN 9781725349445 (ebook)
Subjects: LCSH: Creationism. | Evolution–Religious aspects. | Intelligent design (Teleology)
Classification: LCC BS652.D433 2024 | DDC 231.7'652–dc23

Manufactured in the United States of America
Websites listed were live at the time of publication.

Cover: Romolo Tavani/Shutterstock.com

CPSIA Compliance Information: Batch # SACS24.
For Further Information contact Rosen Publishing at 1-800-237-9932.

CONTENTS

Introduction 6

Section 1: Debating Evolution 7

1.1 When Lord Kelvin Nearly Killed Darwin's Theory 8
By Mano Singham

1.2 The Denialist Playbook 14
By Sean B. Carroll

1.3 On "Darwinism" 23
By Kenneth Miller

1.4 Book Review: God's Word or Human Reason? An Inside Perspective on Creationism 28
By Darren Naish

1.5 Science Denial versus Science Pleasure 33
By Michael Shermer

1.6 Denial of Evolution Is a Form of White Supremacy 36
By Allison Hopper

1.7 Scientists Should Admit They Bring Personal Values to Their Work 40
By Naomi Oreskes

Section 2: Evolution in the Classroom 43

2.1 50 Years Ago: Repeal of Tennessee's "Monkey Law" 44
By Glenn Branch and Ann Reid

2.2 Dissent with Modification: Soothing Evolution-Religion Tensions in the Classroom 47
By Robin Lloyd

2.3 Teachers Help One Another Bring Evolution Back to the Classroom 49
By Adam Piore

2.4 Evolution Is Still True, but ... 63
By Glenn Branch

2.5 Evolution Education in the U.S. Is Getting Better 66
By Glenn Branch and Ann Reid

2.6 Science Education Is Under Legislative Attack 69
By Glenn Branch

Section 3: Evolution Before Our Eyes 72

3.1 That Mouse in Your House—It's Smarter, Thanks to You 73
By Christopher Intagliata

3.2 The Mangrove Finch: An Extinction in Slow Motion 75
By John R. Platt

3.3 Humans Make Wild Animals Less Wary 78
By Jason G. Goldman

3.4 Malaria Mosquitoes Are Biting before Bed-Net Time 80
By Jason G. Goldman

Section 4: Origins of Complex Life 82

4.1 The Noninevitability of Life 83
By Caleb A. Scharf

4.2 The First Gene on Earth May Have Been a Hybrid 86
By Andy Extance

4.3 New Clues about the Origins of Biological Intelligence 91
By Rafael Yuste and Michael Levin

4.4 Evolution's Favorite Fish Diversify through "Noncoding" Genes 96
By Jason G. Goldman

4.5 Fossils Reveal When Animals Started Making Noise 98
By Michael B. Habib

Section 5: Human Evolution 107

5.1 How Scientists Discovered the Staggering Complexity of Human Evolution 108
By Kate Wong

5.2 How a 380-Million-Year-Old Fish Gave Us Fingers 120
By John A. Long and Richard Cloutier

5.3 Fossils Upend Conventional Wisdom about Evolution of Human Bipedalism 132
By Jeremy DeSilva

5.4 Rockshelter Discoveries Show Neandertals Were a Lot like Us 143
By David W. Frayer and Davorka Radovcic

5.5 Mind Your "Fs" and "Vs": Agriculture May Have Shaped Both Human Jaws and Language 152
By Anne Pycha

Glossary 155
Further Information 156
Citations 157
Index 158

INTRODUCTION

Ancient farmers selected the best members of a plant or animal species and encouraged it to reproduce, while preventing other offspring from doing the same. Over time, cattle became larger, wheat became tastier, and cats became pets.

Evolution is a fact of life, not a theory: what Charles Darwin introduced in 1859 was an explanation of how evolution happens. He explained that evolution happens by random chance and environmental pressures, what he called "natural selection." Those members of a species that are better suited to their environment are more likely to pass on their characteristics to the next generation.

In an attempt to reconcile "natural selection" with a belief in a divine creator, some people have looked for evidence that species have always existed as they are today. Others have sought to see in evolution a divine plan. They have fought battles against evolutionary science in the classroom and courtroom. Yet the theory of evolution by natural selection is still a fundamental concept–*the* fundamental concept–in all of the biological sciences. It explains everything from the origins of life on Earth to today's widespread extinctions.

The articles in this book are clearly written from the perspective of that scientific consensus. They are, after all, taken from *Scientific American*. Section 1, "Debating Evolution," puts arguments against evolutionary science under the microscope. Section 2, "Evolution in the Classroom," focuses specifically on the place where evolutionary science is most often challenged. Section 3, "Evolution Before Our Eyes," allows us to see evidence of living species evolving in our own lifetimes. In Section 4, "The Origins of Complex Life," we see Darwin's influence on our understanding the emergence of life on Earth. And Section 5, "Human Evolution," demonstrates that even if our own creation may have taken place over millions of years through random mutations rather than over the course of a day through divine design, it is no less inspiring and humbling to consider.

Section 1: Debating Evolution

1.1 When Lord Kelvin Nearly Killed Darwin's Theory
By Mano Singham

1.2 The Denialist Playbook
By Sean B. Carroll

1.3 On "Darwinism"
By Kenneth Miller

1.4 Book Review: God's Word or Human Reason? An Inside Perspective on Creationism
By Darren Naish

1.5 Science Denial versus Science Pleasure
By Michael Shermer

1.6 Denial of Evolution Is a Form of White Supremacy
By Allison Hopper

1.7 Scientists Should Admit They Bring Personal Values to Their Work
By Naomi Oreskes

When Lord Kelvin Nearly Killed Darwin's Theory

By Mano Singham

The famous opening words, "It was the best of times, it was the worst of times," of Charles Dickens's 1859 novel *A Tale of Two Cities* referred to the period of French Revolution. But he could equally well have been describing his contemporary Charles Darwin's experience with his theory of evolution by natural selection. Darwin was born at the best of times in 1809 when conditions were highly conducive for his theory to flourish, but he died in 1882 at the worst of times because there was a real danger that it might soon be killed off. Darwin's nemesis was the eminent physicist Lord Kelvin, and the weapon used against him was the age of the Earth.

Various theories of evolution predated Darwin, but whatever version one favored, one thing was clear: it needed a very long time for its consequences to work itself out. Precisely how long was hard to pin down, but it was believed to require tens or hundreds of millions of years. From 1650 on, the dominant theory about the age of the Earth, based on the work of Bishop Ussher, Isaac Newton, and many other scholars who used various textual sources, was that it was about 6,000 years.

Theories of geology and biology had to accommodate themselves to this short timeframe. The geological theory known as catastrophism postulated that major features such as the Grand Canyon, Himalayas, etc. had emerged as a result of sudden and violent upheavals. When it came to biological diversity, the idea of special creation, that organisms were immutable and had been specially designed to fit the biological niches in which they found themselves, was the prevailing view.

Such a short window of time would have made it impossible for anyone to credibly propose the emergence of new species by a process of slow evolution. But around 1785, ideas of the age of the Earth began to undergo a radical change as geologists and paleontologists started using the features of the Earth itself, such as erosion, sedimentation, and the layers of strata and the fossils embedded in them, to estimate its age. The theory of uniformitarianism, that major geological features were caused by the very slow accumulation of tiny changes, gained ground, culminating in Charles Lyell's epic three-volume work *Principles of Geology* in 1830, which cemented the idea that the Earth had been around for hundreds of millions of years and possibly much longer, so long that it seemed impossible to fix an actual age.

Darwin was also a keen student of geology and was familiar with Lyell's work (they later became close friends) and had the first two volumes of his book with him as he made his five-year voyage around the globe on the HMS *Beagle* during 1831–1836, where the ideas for his theory of evolution germinated as he observed the patterns of species in the various locations that he visited. Darwin knew from his work with pigeons that even deliberately breeding for specific characteristics took a long time to produce them. But how much time was necessary? He felt that it required at least hundreds of millions of years. The work of Lyell and other geologists gave him the luxury of assuming that sufficient time existed for natural selection to do its work.

Darwin also came of age at a time when the idea that species were immutable had begun to crumble. While Darwin was taught and accepted the still dominant special creation theory, he was also familiar with the general idea of evolution. His own grandfather Erasmus Darwin had in 1794 published a book *Zoonomia* that explored proto-evolutionary ideas. Jean-Baptiste Lamarck had published his own model of how evolution worked in 1802. The various models proposed for the mechanism of evolution, such as Lamarckian evolution, orthogenesis, and use-disuse, all implied some level of teleology: that there was a directionality inherent in the process.

The extremely long window of time opened up by the new geology allowed Darwin and his co-creator Alfred Russell Wallace, working independently, to develop the central new insight of natural selection that differed from other models of evolution by showing how diversity could arise naturally by a process of Malthusian population selection pressures, without any kind of mystical agency directing the process towards any specific ends.

Their theory held that evolution was contingency-driven in that how organisms evolved depended on chance factors and a changing environment, which suggested that if we ran the clock again, we could get very different outcomes in which human beings might never appear. Their work was first presented in a joint paper in 1858. Darwin's major work *On the Origin of Species*, published a year later, was a closely argued compilation of a massive amount of evidence that helped establish evolution as a fact.

The radical change in the status of human beings implied by their model, from being specially created in the image of God to just another accidental byproduct of the evolutionary process just like all other species, was an immediate source of controversy because it challenged a key religious tenet that human beings were special. This was why natural selection aroused such opposition even while evolution was accepted. Many scientists of that time were religious and believed in theistic evolution that said that a supernatural agency was guiding the process to produce the desired ends.

While all models of evolution required long times, *natural* selection required much longer times than any *guided* selection process. Hence the younger the age of the Earth, the more likely it was that natural selection could not be the mechanism. Physicists, led by the eminent Kelvin, himself a theistic evolutionist, were leaders of the charge for a young Earth, though it must be emphasized that "young" at that time meant around 100 million years or less. Even religious scientists had abandoned the idea of the Earth being just 6,000 years old.

Beginning around 1860, Kelvin and other physicists started estimating the ages of the Earth and sun using the nebular hypothesis proposed around 1750 by Immanuel Kant and Pierre-Simon Laplace. This model treated the Earth and the sun as starting as rotating clouds of particles that coalesced under gravity to form molten balls, with the Earth subsequently solidifying and cooling. Kelvin used the laws of thermodynamics and other physics principles to arrive at estimates of 20–400 million years. By 1879 the upper limit had been lowered to about 100 million years for the Earth and an even shorter upper limit of 20 million years for the Sun, much less than the 200 million years or so believed to be required for natural selection to work. Since physics was considered to be the most rigorous of the sciences, things looked bad for natural selection.

When Darwin died in 1882, he was mourned as a great scientist who had radically changed our understanding of how the vast diversity of organisms we see around us came about, dethroning the idea that they were immutable. But because of the shrinking age of the Earth, he died with a major cloud hanging over his mechanism of natural selection. Darwin's final words on the topic, written in 1880 just two years before his death, expressed a plaintive hope that future developments might reconcile the needs of natural selection with physics calculations:

> With respect to the lapse of time not having been sufficient since our planet was consolidated for the assumed amount of organic change, and this objection, as urged by [Lord Kelvin], is probably one of the gravest as yet advanced, I can only say, firstly that we do not know at what rate species change as measured in years, and secondly that many philosophers are not yet willing to admit that we know enough of the constitution of the universe and of the interior of our globe to speculate with safety on its past duration.

It turned out Darwin was prescient that improved knowledge of the interior of the Earth might change the calculations in his favor, but at the time he seemed to be grasping at straws. In fact, in the near term the problem got even worse because Kelvin and others produced new calculations that resulted in the age of the Earth being reduced even more, so that by 1895 the consensus physics view was that the age of the planet lay in the range 20–40 million years. Natural selection appeared to be doomed.

But physicists were now encountering stiffer opposition from other disciplines. Geologists were adamant that their models based on the accumulating evidence on sedimentation and erosion, while not as rigorous as the physics models, were well enough established that they were confident of their lower limit of 100 million years. Paleontologists were also arguing that the fossil record was not consistent with the physicists' shorter ages. Both groups argued that the physicists must have gone awry somewhere, even if they could not point out the specific flaws.

Beginning in 1895, this impasse began to be broken when physicist John Perry, a former assistant of Kelvin's, challenged the latter's assumption that the Earth was a rigid and homogeneous body, saying there was little evidence to support it. By introducing inhomogeneity and convective flow in the Earth's interior, he found that Kelvin's estimates for the age of the Earth could change by as much as a factor as 100, shifting the upper limit into the billions of years. Other physicists also chimed in with similar upward shifts, and this encouraged geologists, paleontologists and biologists to ignore the physicists' arguments for a young Earth.

It was the discovery of radioactivity that decisively changed the picture; it led to an entirely new way of measuring the age of the Earth, by allowing scientists to calculate the ages of rocks. Since the oldest rock that could be found set a lower limit for the age of the Earth, the race was on to find older and older rocks using this method; records fell rapidly, leading to ages of 141 million years by 1905, 1.64 billion years by 1911, 1.9 billion years by 1935, 3.35 billion years by 1947, and to 4.5 billion years by 1953, which is where the current consensus lies.

When Kelvin died in 1907 at the age of 83, it was not clear if he had accepted that his estimates were no longer valid. But Darwin's hope that Kelvin would be proven wrong, and that eventually it would be shown that sufficient time existed for natural selection to work, was realized, 30 years after Darwin's death. His theory now has all the time it needs.

This is an opinion and analysis article; the views expressed by the author or authors are not necessarily those of Scientific American.

About the Author

Mano Singham is a Fellow of the American Physical Society and the retired director of the University Center for Innovation in Teaching and Education and adjunct associate professor of Physics at Case Western Reserve University. His latest book is The Great Paradox of Science: Why its conclusions can be relied upon even though they cannot be proven *(Oxford University Press).*

The Denialist Playbook

By Sean B. Carroll

Once upon a time, in a land not far away, there was a horrible virus that instilled terror in every town and home. Although most people who became infected showed no symptoms or recovered within a week, in a small fraction of cases the illness progressed, causing loss of reflexes and muscle control, paralysis and, sometimes, death.

Children were especially vulnerable, so parents watched anxiously for any sign of infection, often keeping them away from swimming pools, movie theaters, bowling alleys, anywhere where there were crowds and the dreaded microbe might lurk. Travel and business were sometimes curtailed between places with outbreaks, and public health authorities imposed quarantines on healthy people who may have been exposed, in order to halt the spread of the disease. In the first half of the 1950s, with no cure and no vaccine, more than 200,000 Americans were disabled by the poliovirus. The virus was second only to the atomic bomb as to what Americans feared most.

Then, on April 12, 1955, public health officials at the University of Michigan announced that a "safe, effective, and potent" vaccine had been found. This set off a national celebration that recalled the end of World War II. Church bells rang, car horns honked, people wept with relief. President Eisenhower invited the vaccine's inventor, Jonas Salk, to the White House. In a Rose Garden ceremony, the former Supreme Allied Commander told the scientist in a trembling voice, "I should like to say to you that when I think of the countless thousands of American parents and grandparents who are hereafter to be spared the agonizing fears of the annual epidemic of poliomyelitis, when I think of all the agony that these people will be spared seeing their loved ones suffering in bed, I must say to you I have no words in which adequately to express the thanks of myself and all the people I know–all 164 million Americans, to say nothing of all the people in the world that will profit from your discovery."

But, alas, not everyone joined the party and expressed such gratitude. One group in particular did not welcome the vaccine as a breakthrough. Chiropractors actively opposed the vaccination campaign that followed Salk's triumph. Many practitioners dismissed the role of contagious pathogens and adhered to the founding principle of chiropractic that all disease originated in the spine. Just a few years after the introduction of the vaccine, as the number of polio cases was declining rapidly, an article in the *Journal of the National Chiropractic Association* asked, "Has the Test Tube Fight Against Polio Failed?" It recommended that, rather than take the vaccine, once stricken, "Chiropractic adjustments should be given of the entire spine during the first three days of polio."

Opposition to the polio vaccine and to vaccination in general continued in the ranks such that even four decades later, long after polio had been eradicated from the United States, as many as one third of chiropractors still believed that there was no scientific proof that vaccination prevents any disease, including polio. That belief and resistance continues to this day, with some chiropractors campaigning against state vaccination mandates.

I was shocked when I first learned about chiropractors' opposition to the polio vaccine. The vaccine is widely viewed as one of medicine's greatest success stories: Why would anyone have opposed it? My shock turned into excitement, however, when I began to recognize the chiropractors' pattern of arguments was uncannily similar to those I was familiar with from creationists who deny evolutionary science. And once I perceived those parallels, my excitement became an epiphany when I realized that the same general pattern of arguments—a denialist playbook—has been deployed to reject other scientific consensuses from the health effects of tobacco to the existence and causes of climate change. The same playbook is now being used to deny facts concerning the COVID-19 pandemic.

In brief, the six principal plays in the denialist playbook are:

- Doubt the Science
- Question Scientists' Motives and Integrity

- Magnify Disagreements among Scientists and Cite Gadflies as Authorities
- Exaggerate Potential Harm
- Appeal to Personal Freedom
- Reject Whatever Would Repudiate a Key Philosophy

The purpose of the denialism playbook is to advance rhetorical arguments that give the appearance of legitimate debate when there is none. My purpose here is to penetrate that rhetorical fog, and to show that these are the predictable tactics of those clinging to an untenable position. If we hope to find any cure for (or vaccine against) science denialism, scientists, journalists and the public need to be able recognize, understand and anticipate these plays.

To illustrate how the playbook works–and sadly, it is very effective –I will break down the chiropractor and creationist versions, which have endured for many decades in spite of overwhelming evidence, and point out parallels to the coronavirus rhetoric.

The Playbook

1. Doubt the Science

The first tactic of denialism is to raise objections to scientific evidence or interpretations. This may take the form of seemingly legitimate specific arguments against a scientific claim. For example, chiropractors sought other explanations besides vaccine efficacy to account for the decline of infectious diseases: "The Center for Disease Control statistics make it clear that the majority of diseases that are now routinely vaccinated against were disappearing before either the cause was discovered or the vaccine developed," stated a 1995 letter to the editor of *Dynamic Chiropractic* magazine. In polio's case, this argument does not hold up against the facts that: (a) the disease was surging in the 1950s; (b) the vaccine was proven effective in a massive double-blind, placebo-controlled trial;

and (c) infections declined precipitously after the introduction of the vaccine.

Alternatively, some statements are blanket arguments against an entire scientific discipline. For example, Henry Morris, whose 1961 book *The Genesis Flood* is credited with reviving the creationism movement, alleged: "Since there is no real scientific evidence that evolution is occurring at present or ever occurred in the past, it is reasonable to conclude that evolution is not a fact of science, as many claim. In fact, it is not even science at all, but an arbitrary system built upon faith in universal naturalism."

2. Question Scientists' Motives and Integrity

As a growing body of consistent evidence can be hard to explain away, one fallback is to impugn the source. In the vaccination arena, this often takes the form of alleging financial conflicts of interest on the part of scientists, greed on the part of manufacturers, and complicity of government officials. "It appears that the scientific foundation on which these vaccines have been erected is fragile enough that only compulsory laws, expensive public relations efforts, outrageous propaganda, and expensive advertising must ensue for compliance to be maintained," wrote one author in *American Chiropractor*. Salk, by the way, filed no patent.

In the evolution arena, scientists are often accused of being part of a conspiracy to undermine religion through educational systems. Kenneth Cumming, of the Institute for Creation Research, objected to a PBS series on evolution by drawing a parallel to the 9/11 attackers: "America is being attacked from within through its public schools by a militant religious movement of philosophical naturalists (i.e., atheists) under the guise of secular Darwinism. Both desire to alter the life and thinking of our nation." One noteworthy counter to such assertions is the Clergy Letter Project, which has gained the support of more than 15,000 Christian clergy for the teaching of evolution.

3. Magnify Disagreements among Scientists and Cite Gadflies as Authorities

In all scientific arenas, there is honest disagreement about the interpretation of evidence. However, these differences are deliberately inflated by denialists to imply a lack of consensus on more fundamental points, while often propounding the contradictory views of a few unqualified outliers. An example of the latter is how some chiropractors have seized on the anti-vaccination stance of one critic, Viera Scheibner. Her claim that there is no evidence for vaccine efficacy or safety is cited repeatedly, while overlooking the fact that her training and expertise is in geology, not medicine.

In the evolution arena, differences of interpretation among scientists are relished by anti-evolution voices. For example, the initial discovery of a new fossil hominid usually elicits some different interpretations and expressions of uncertainty in the scientific community. Creationists often mischaracterize these normal dynamics of scientific discourse as "skepticism" over the significance of such finds so as to discount them. By overblowing legitimate disagreements and propounding "alternatives" to evolution, denialists often make appeals to "teach the controversy," when no such controversy exists in the scientific community. Different interpretations of a fossil do not negate the discomfiting evidence for the antiquity of human ancestors.

Anti-evolution leaders in the U.S. also include a small number of scholars whose credentials are in other disciplines. For example, the above-mentioned Henry Morris was an engineer, not a biologist. Phillip E. Johnson, whose book *Darwin on Trial* inspired many adherents to the intelligent design movement, was a law professor with no formal training in biology.

A lack of credentials or status within the scientific community is often seen not as a liability but as a virtue. Scientists Pascal Diethelm and Martin McKee note, "Denialists are usually not deterred by the extreme isolation of their theories, but rather see it as the indication of their intellectual courage against the dominant orthodoxy and the accompanying political correctness, often comparing themselves to Galileo."

4. Exaggerate Potential Harm

When the evidence contradicts a position, another recourse is to try to incite fear. No vaccine or medicine is 100 percent safe, without any risk of side effects. Chiropractors have long emphasized the potential side effects of vaccines, for example in a statement in *Dynamic Chiropractic* offering a litany of possible effects: "death, encephalopathy, demyelinating diseases, brachial neuritis, Guillain-Barré syndrome, infections generated by vaccine agents, anaphylaxis, subacute sclerosing panencephalitis, seizure disorder, optic neuritis, arthritis," and so on. However, they generally fail to acknowledge the serious consequences of infections that would be prevented by vaccination.

But what harm could arise from knowing a bit about evolution? Well, Hitler, of course! "Of the many factors that produced the Nazi Holocaust and World War II," wrote one critic in the *Journal of Creation*, "one of the most important was Darwin's notion that evolutionary progress occurs mainly as a result of the elimination of the weak in the struggle for survival." It is an oft-repeated argument that has no bearing of course on the veracity of Darwin's theory.

Vaccination foes have lobbed similar accusations, likening physicians who administer vaccines to Nazi doctors and alleging that vaccines violate the 1947 Nuremberg Code of medical ethics.

5. Appeal to Personal Freedom

If fear is not persuasive, there is another fallback position that resonates strongly with Americans: the freedom of choice. The American Chiropractic Association leaned on this cherished notion when it established its official vaccination policy:

> Since the scientific community acknowledges that the use of vaccines is not without risk, the American Chiropractic Association

> supports each individual's right to freedom of choice in his/her own health care based on an informed awareness of the benefits and possible adverse effects of vaccination. The ACA is supportive of a conscience clause or waiver in compulsory vaccination laws... providing an elective course of action regarding vaccination.

Likewise, the International Chiropractic Association "questions the wisdom of mass vaccination programs" and views compulsory programs as an infringement of "the individual's right to freedom of choice."

Similarly, the teaching of evolution in public schools is viewed as an assault upon the religious freedom of those who oppose it. Those holding this view advocate for disclaimers on textbooks ("just a theory"), the teaching of "alternative" views of the history of life (Genesis or intelligent design), or the freedom to opt out of the evolution curriculum of biology classes.

Notably, the U.S. Supreme Court has rejected challenges to compulsory vaccination partly on the grounds that individual belief cannot subordinate the safety of an entire community. And U.S. courts have repeatedly struck down attempts to subvert the teaching of evolution as religiously motivated and violations of the establishment clause of the First Amendment of the U.S. Constitution.

6. Reject Whatever Would Repudiate a Key Philosophy

Once the courts have spoken, and the scientific evidence grows to be overwhelming, one might think that denialists would be out of plays. But there is one last line of defense that reveals the nucleus of denial: It is not that some scientific claim is untrue; it is that it is unacceptable in light of some philosophical commitment. The science must be summarily rejected.

Chiropractic was founded in the early 20th century on the assertion that all disease has its origins in misalignments of the spine. "Chiropractors have found in every disease that is supposed to be contagious, a cause in the spine," claimed Bartlett Joshua Palmer, the son of chiropractic founder Daniel David Palmer. Acceptance of germ theory and vaccination would repudiate the founding premise of the profession that all disease stems from vertebral misalignments. Therefore, that premise cannot be questioned.

With respect to evolution, Henry Morris made it plain: "When science and the Bible differ, science has obviously misinterpreted its data."

Any credence granted to evolutionary science is a threat to a worldview based on interpretation of the Bible; David Cloud, a publisher of Bible study materials argues: "If the Bible does not mean what it says, there is no way to know what it does mean.

Historian of science and author Naomi Oreskes has coined a term for this stance: "implicatory denial"–the rejection of scientific findings because we don't like their implications.

As these positions are reinforced by family or community, they harden into part of one's identity. "In this way, cultural identity starts to override facts," Norwegian climate psychologist Per Espen Stoknes has said. "And my identity trumps truth any day."

Psychologists Elliot Aronson and Carol Tavris write in the *Atlantic*: "[W]hen people feel a strong connection to a political party, leader, ideology, or belief, they are more likely to let that allegiance do their thinking for them and distort or ignore the evidence that challenges those loyalties."

The denialist playbook is now erupting around the coronavirus. Although COVID-19 is new, the reactions to public health measures, scientific claims, and expert advice are not. Attitudes and behaviors concerning the threat posed by the coronavirus (doubting the science), the efficacy of lockdowns and mask wearing (freedoms being eroded) and alternative treatments (gadflies over experts) are being driven as much or more by rhetoric than by evidence.

Polls indicate that despite the devastating health and economic impacts of the pandemic, with respect to a potential vaccine we are nowhere near as united as Americans were in 1955. But as epidemiologist Michael Osterholm noted in June, 2020, "Eventually there won't be any blue states or red states. There won't be any blue cities or red rural areas. It'll all be COVID colored."

Now, sadly, there is no denying that.

About the Author

Sean B. Carroll is Distinguished University Professor of Biology at the University of Maryland and vice president for science education at the Howard Hughes Medical Institute. His latest book is A Series of Fortunate Events: Chance the Making of the Planet Life *(Princeton University Press).*

On "Darwinism"

By Kenneth Miller

He could have just said he didn't believe in evolution, or that evolution had flaws. Or, he could have said that a book with a whole unit on evolution was just too much. But William Buckingham, of the Dover Area School Board in Pennsylvania, didn't use the "E" word when he explained his objections to the biology textbook selected by the science teachers at Dover High School. Instead, he invoked a term that didn't even appear in that textbook. Prentice Hall's *Biology: The Living Science*, he claimed, "was laced with *Darwinism* from beginning to end." Surely, he must have thought, "Darwinism" was a disqualifying slander that everyone could understand.

As he explained his remarks to a reporter, Buckingham expanded on that theme, once again invoking the name of Darwin rather than the name of the field itself. "It's okay to teach Darwin," said Buckingham, "but you have to balance it with something else, such as creationism." Later that year, the school board attempted to do exactly that, pairing "Darwinism" with "Intelligent Design," and leading to the landmark *Kitzmiller v. Dover* trial in 2005. The defenders of evolution won a resounding victory in that trial, but afterwards I was left to wonder how Darwin's own name had come to be used as a slur against science.

To find the intellectual roots of that transformation, one need look no further than a 1998 essay by one of America's greatest living writers, Marilynne Robinson. Author of novels such as *Housekeeping, Home* and *Gilead*, for which she won the Pulitzer Prize in 2005, Robinson is also the author of "Darwinism," a provocative essay that forms the cornerstone of her 1998 collection of essays, *The Death of Adam*. Robinson is no creationist. In fact, she writes that creationism, a "caricature of religion," is "the best thing that could have happened to Darwinism," since it "justifies Darwinist contempt for the whole of religion." What, then, is her objection to evolution?

Surprisingly, she does not seem to have one, at least not a scientific objection. In fact, she regards Darwin's work as "impressive," and makes no argument for a young Earth, the fixity of species or any of the other usual creationist canards. But to her mind, "Darwinism" is something else again. She writes that Charles Darwin had a "cheerful interest" in the extermination of races, that "Darwinism is harsh and crude," and that Darwinists regard the human animal as a "creature who shares essential attributes with whatever beast has recently been observed behaving shabbily in the state of nature."

Robinson makes no case for the existence of a historical Adam or the Garden of Eden, but she clearly laments the way in which evolution, or "Darwinism," has dispelled the civilizing myth of Adam, and the key "assumptions" that once formed the bedrock of Western culture, even the culture of science itself. If one were to seek an intellectual founding mother for the use of "Darwinism" as a slander against evolution, Robinson would surely get that honor.

A number of purposes are served by reducing an entire scientific field to an "ism" based on the name of its founder. The first is obvious. Evolution then becomes an ideology, not a field of science. This view is on full display at the lavishly appointed Creation Museum in Petersburg, Kentucky, where visitors are assured that scientific data can be interpreted in two ways—from a Darwinist perspective, or from a creationist point of view. Because both depend only upon one's preconceptions, the creationist viewpoint is just as valid as any other.

Like any supposed ism, Darwinism has an agenda, and it's not just a scientific one. It dismisses moral values as the epiphenomena of natural selection, it promotes homosexuality, ruthless competition, selfishness and racism, and it seeks to explain the gems of western civilization, its art, music and literature, as nothing more than individual gambits that advance the artist's own interests in sex and reproduction. These supposed evils derive from the way in which it advances a strictly materialistic view of nature, one that, in Robinson's words, "denies the mind/soul as spirit," and regards the brain as nothing more than a "lump of meat." Darwinism requires "the disengagement of conscience," and the "grand scale disparagement of the traits that distinguish us from animals." And Darwinists, she notes, "take the darkest possible view of the animals."

The overuse of Darwin's own name facilitates another line of attack, by pretending that the field relies entirely on Darwin's own work, fashioned in an age before the modern sciences of genetics, biochemistry and molecular biology emerged to confirm and expand his ideas. This allows the pretense that evolution is a stolid, unchanging field, with few new ideas that might refresh its 19th century heritage. Any scientist would scoff at this, of course, knowing the vigor that new discoveries constantly infuse into evolutionary biology. But to laypeople, unfamiliar with the rapid pace of scientific discovery, this can be a persuasive argument.

Finally, by constantly railing against pernicious "Darwinism," the advocate can map the many personal faults and flaws of Charles Darwin and his like-minded contemporaries onto evolution itself. Darwin's racism is thereby presumed to be inherent to the field, as is the imperial condescension that might be found in any upper-class Briton of the period. Closer to the present day, the eugenics movement can be linked to Darwinism as well, misrepresenting the science of evolution as justification for the horrors inflicted in its name.

What, then, is to be done? Should we abstain from the use of Darwin's name, stop reading *The Origin of Species* or co-opt the term by applying it broadly to evolutionary science? While I don't think that's necessary, we should keep in mind that many of our professional colleagues have indeed attached the authority of evolution to assertions that are more political and cultural than biological. One such field is evolutionary psychology, a discipline in which evolutionary principles can indeed be used to great effect. But it is also a field in which Darwinian "just-so" arguments have been used to explain everything from male and female shopping behavior to music and to tell us that the impulse to rape was favored by natural selection–so all males are potential rapists. A gentler example of this cultural overreach is proudly advanced by David

Sloan Wilson, president of the Evolution Institute, who proclaims that in this century the theory of evolution will expand "to include all human-related knowledge," including "anthropology, art, culture, economics, history, politics, psychology, religion, and sociology." In short, step aside, humanists and social scientists, we're taking over.

Maybe so. But I'm still waiting for an evolutionary explanation of the thrilling beauty of a Mozart symphony or a James Joyce short story, to say nothing of a truly biological explanation for the particular political situations in the U.S., Venezuela or Germany. In advocating for greater public understanding of evolution, we might do well to keep in mind that it is a theory for the origin of species, not the explanation of all things human, great and small.

But there is a deeper, more powerful strategy that can get to the very heart of the fundamental concerns of intellectuals like Robinson and laypeople who share her concern that evolution diminishes the status of the human person. That is to use evolution itself to highlight the exceptional nature of our species. Yes, there was an element of truth in Henry Gee's admonition that "There is nothing special about being human, any more than there is anything special about being a guinea pig or a geranium." Frans de Waal made a similar point regarding the human intellect. We are, he asserted, "animals not only in body but also in mind." Science blogger P. Z. Myers was even more explicit in his efforts to take us down a notch: "we [humans] aren't any more special to the universe than a sea slug." While all of these statements emphasize our full-fledged membership in the animal kingdom, they miss something–something essential to a genuine understanding of the place our species holds in the evolutionary narrative.

Referring to the work of two great pioneers of animal behavior, the late Jacob Bronowski wryly pointed out that their studies of birds and rodents fell somewhat short of accounting for the most important details of human behavior: "There must be something unique about man because otherwise, evidently, the ducks would be lecturing about Konrad Lorenz, and the rats would be writing papers about B. F. Skinner." That is exactly the point.

We are the children of evolution in every sense, part of Darwin's fabled "tangled bank." We must never forget that. But we must also remember that we are the only creatures to emerge from that thicket and make sense of it all. "Darwinism" does not diminish us. Rather, it puts the human experiment into a truly scientific perspective. We are not just hairless bipedal primates. We are creatures capable of the fugues of Bach, the verses of Yeats, the stories of Twain, the creations of Dalí and, for that matter, the mathematics of Gödel, Ramanujan and Turing.

In contemplating the lessons of evolution for our species and our culture, this is how we should overcome the mindless use of "Darwinism" as a slur. Some may feel demeaned by our evolutionary heritage, but I would argue that the more appropriate emotions are joy and delight. Joy that we are approaching a genuine understanding of the world in which we live, and delight at being the very first stirrings of true consciousness in the vastness of the cosmos. Far from diminishing us, knowing the details of Adam's journey ennobles each of us as a carrier of something truly precious–the genetic, biological, and cultural heritage of life itself. Evolution describes not the death of Adam, but his triumph. That is the great truth of our story.

The views expressed are those of the author(s) and are not necessarily those of Scientific American.

About the Author

Kenneth Miller is a professor of biology at Brown University and the author, most recently, of The Human Instinct.

Book Review: God's Word or Human Reason? An Inside Perspective on Creationism

By Darren Naish

A vast amount of evidence–encompassing virtually every subject in the natural sciences–demonstrates that our planet has a long, complex history, that life emerged following chemical innovations involving self-replicating molecules, and that the vast panoply of organisms living and extinct owe their existence to a gradual process in which changes are heritable and descendants become ever more distinct from their forebears. Yet significant sectors of the population in many parts of the world ignore or reject this view and rely instead on strict interpretations of religious texts. Is there a contradiction between religion and an evolutionary, Old Earth view of the natural world? While this varies from one religion to the next, scarcely any religion is specific enough to contradict, in detail, our scientific understanding of life, history, Earth and the universe as it has developed over recent centuries.

Jonathan Kane, Emily Willoughby, and T. Michael Keesey's 2016 *God's Word or Human Reason? An Inside Perspective on Creationism* had its beginnings in the 2007 opening of the Answers in Genesis (AiG) Creation Museum of Petersburg, Kentucky. So much media coverage and so much apparent interest was generated by this event that–so Kane, Willoughby, and Keesey realised–clear and comprehensive response was warranted. A book was the only workable solution. And this book needed to cover geological history and dating, a review of "flood geology," and reviews of our knowledge on dinosaurs and hominids, all areas that AiG mangles and distorts via its many Young Earth Creationist (YEC) claims. Further, AiG's specific brand of young Earth creationism is so wrought and peculiar that effective counter requires insider knowledge and experience of the YEC literature, which is quite the thing to behold and little known, or unknown, to the majority of mainstream scientists.

The title of this book–*God's Word or Human Reason?*–is a response to AiG's opening gambit: that the evolutionary, Old Earth view of science is merely the product of "human reason" (AiG's specific term), and that we do better to reject it in favour of accepting "God's word" (again, AiG's specific term).

Yet, as Kane explains in Chapter 1, a religious Christian view would be that human reason is a gift from God, that God has left copious data by which we can evaluate the formation of the universe, the Earth, and the living things upon it, and that the Bible itself has long been established contradictory with evidence.

This book, then, does not set out to convert any Christian to atheism, nor is it hostile or unfriendly to Christianity or religion in general. While an atheist or non-Christian of any sort will find the book good and useful, it is predominantly written for Christians such that they appreciate the lack of contradiction between Christian faith and scientific knowledge, all the while denouncing the peculiar take promoted by AiG and YEC in general.

It has been said many times in the battle against the lies and mis-education of the creationists that among the most important opponents of YEC are those who were once YECs themselves. And here's the kicker, because all the contributing authors of *God's Word or Human Reason?* (there are five) are exactly that. Testimonials provided by each explain what it was that led them to doubt, question and ultimately reject YEC. These personal stories are fascinating, in one case heartbreaking.

As a physical object, this book is spectacularly well designed, with a size, feel and format that I really admire. The picture-to-text ratio (a non-trivial feature of design that is rarely mentioned but, in my experience, crucial to how we feel about works of scientific literature) is very near perfect, there being relatively few places where more than four consecutive pages lack illustrations of some sort. The quality of editing is extremely high and typos are few.

As for the contents themselves, six chapters cover, variously, the nature of science and evolutionary theory (Kane, Chapter 1); the flood and the fossil record (Glenn Morton, Chapter 2); radiometric dating and the age of the Earth (Willoughby, Chapter 3); created kinds and the origin of birds (Kane, Chapter 4); human evolution (Keesey, Chapter 5); and how we should interpret the Bible (James Comer, Chapter 6).

The scene is set with an introduction that covers the nature of the problem, the USA's exceptionalism and the problem as exemplified by the views of congressmen and other politicians. The stated aim is to challenge and show wrong the claims of AiG; to demonstrate how AiG's arguments are transparently inconsistent with easily understood evidence, presented here in abundant detail. Indeed, the chapters are thorough, well crafted and fantastically well researched.

Kane's review of what we currently think about the evolution of birds from among theropod dinosaurs, for example, is one of the best reviews of this area yet published, combining historical review with a tour of key taxa in the "theropod to bird" transition. The fact that fossil discoveries repeatedly *matched predictions* made about the evolutionary history of this group of animals is rightly emphasized. And what, then, of the AiG claim that the existence of a discrete "dinosaur kind" and "bird kind" is consistent with creationism, not evolution? (creationists use the term "baramin" for these discrete "created kinds").

Anyone actually aware of the large number of near-bird and early bird fossils discovered recently in the Jurassic and Cretaceous rocks of eastern Asia and elsewhere will be familiar with the fact that these animals are all–phylogenetically and metaphorically speaking– "shades of grey" as goes any imagined boundary between "dinosaurs" and "birds," but the fun part for our discussion here is that *even creationists themselves* have announced this finding when they've used statistical techniques to determine the anatomical distance between the animals involved. Yes, a small field of creationist study termed *baraminology* aims to assert–I mean *test*–the difference between baramins.

My favorite chapter–in that I found it most surprising and interesting, I guess–is, somewhat ironically, Glenn Morton's on flood geology, in part because I hadn't heard the full inside story on creationist interpretations of flood geology in such detail before (I say "somewhat ironically" only because geology is lower on my list of interests than dinosaurs and hominids). Besides marshalling the substantial evidence that counts against the existence of a global flood, Morton draws attention to the massive inconsistency present across YEC literature as YECs have struggled to account for geological and taphonomic evidence. And, as Morton shows, the wording in the Bible doesn't require a global flood anyway.

I also need to give special mention to T. Michael Keesey's fantastic and very long chapter on hominids. Again, the AiG idea that the fossils of this group are either "fully ape" or "fully human" is transparently contradicted by the anatomical evidence. Rarely has such a quantity of information on the evidence linking humans with other apes been presented; Keesey discusses features of the integumentary, circulatory, nervous and skeletal system that tie humans to other apes before going on to review the hominin fossil record. The chapter is richly illustrated with images of fossils, graphs, maps, cladograms and silhouette reconstructions of the taxa involved. Those specially interested in the hominin fossil record should get the book for this chapter alone.

Appendices list those feathered dinosaurs relevant to Chapter 4 and the numerous traits (present across all biological systems) shared by humans and other apes, and relevant to Chapter 5. A substantial glossary and bibliography are included, and the book is fully indexed. The text is also highly up to date and fully and thoroughly referenced (Chapter 4 contains 300 citations; Chapter 5 a whopping 436).

All in all, I cannot recommend this book highly enough. As an educational outreach tool to Christians interested in learning about evolution and seeing evaluations and checks of the many doubtful or wrong claims made by AiG it is essential. But it is also just a very useful, very interesting book to people of any sort interested in evolution and approaches to it, and the reviews it includes are really strong. It is also very reasonably priced given its size and technical quality.

Finally, it is clearly worthy and essential that Christian creationism be tackled, deconstructed and countered, and that its impact on education, public policy and social welfare be minimised. But Christian creationism is not the only brand of creationism that exists, nor are Christians the only community of people where creationist worldviews are common, nor are Christians like Ken Ham the only ones indulging in noisy promotion of anti-evolutionary rhetoric. I refer, of course, to Islamic creationism, and in particular to the highly dishonest writings of Harun Yahya (real name Adnan Oktar). Concerns about Islamic creationism have been prominent for years—in Turkey in particular—but how soon will it be before a volume, written for Muslims and countering Oktar's many claims, appears in print?

The views expressed are those of the author(s) and are not necessarily those of Scientific American.

Referenced

Kane, J. 2016a. Chapter 1. God's word or human reason? In Kane, J., Willoughby, E. & Keesey, T. M. *God's Word or Human Reason? An Inside Perspective on Creationism.* Inkwater Press, pp. 1-11.

Kane, J. 2016b. Chapter 4. Created kinds and the origin of birds. In Kane, J., Willoughby, E. & Keesey, T. M. *God's Word or Human Reason? An Inside Perspective on Creationism*. Inkwater Press, pp. 105-180.

Senter, P. 2011. Using creation science to demonstrate evolution 2: morphological continuity within Dinosauria. *Journal of Evolutionary Biology* 24, 2197-2216.

About the Author

Darren Naish is a science writer, technical editor and palaeozoologist (affiliated with the University of Southampton, UK). He mostly works on Cretaceous dinosaurs and pterosaurs but has an avid interest in all things tetrapod. His publications can be downloaded at darrennaish.wordpress.com. He has been blogging at Tetrapod Zoology since 2006.

Science Denial versus Science Pleasure

By Michael Shermer

That conservatives doubt scientific findings and theories that conflict with their political and religious beliefs is evident from even a cursory scan of right-leaning media. The denial of evolution and of global warming and the pushback against stem cell research are the most egregious examples in recent decades. It is not surprising, because we expect those on the right to let their politics trump science—tantamount to a dog-bites-man story.

That liberals are just as guilty of anti-science bias comports more with accounts of humans chomping canines, and yet those on the left are just as skeptical of well-established science when findings clash with their political ideologies, such as with GMOs, nuclear power, genetic engineering and evolutionary psychology—skepticism of the last I call "cognitive creationism" for its endorsement of a blank-slate model of the mind in which natural selection operated on humans only from the neck down.

In reality, anti-science attitudes are formed in very narrow cognitive windows—those in which science appears to oppose certain political or religious views. Most people embrace most of science most of the time.

Who is skeptical of science, then, and when?

That question was the title of an October 2017 talk I attended by Asheley R. Landrum, a psychologist at Texas Tech University, who studies factors influencing the public understanding and perception of science, health and emerging technologies. She began by citing surveys that found more than 90 percent of both Republicans and Democrats agreed that "science and technology give more opportunities" and that "science makes our lives better." She also reviewed modest evidence in support of the "knowledge deficit hypothesis," which posits that public skepticism of science is the result of inadequate scientific knowledge. Those who know more about climate science, for example, are slightly more likely to accept that global warming is real and caused by humans than those who know less on the subject.

But that modest effect not only is erased when political ideology is factored in, it has an opposite effect on one end of the political spectrum. For Republicans, the more knowledge they have about climate science the *less likely* they are to accept the theory of anthropogenic global warming (whereas Democrats' confidence goes up). "People with more knowledge only accept science when it doesn't conflict with their preexisting beliefs and values," Landrum explained. "Otherwise, they use that knowledge to more strongly justify their own positions."

Landrum and her colleagues demonstrated the effect experimentally and reported the results in a 2017 paper in the *Journal of Risk Research* entitled "Culturally Antagonistic Memes and the Zika Virus: An Experimental Test," in which participants read a news story on Zika public health risks that was linked to either climate change or immigration. Predictably, when Zika was connected to climate change, there was an increase in concern among Democrats and a decrease in concern among Republicans, but when Zika was associated with immigration, the effects were reversed. Skepticism, it would seem, is context-dependent. "We are good at being skeptical when information conflicts with our preexisting beliefs and values," Landrum noted. "We are bad at being skeptical when information is compatible with our preexisting beliefs and values."

In another 2017 study published in *Advances in Political Psychology*, "Science Curiosity and Political Information Processing," Landrum and her colleagues found that liberal Democrats were far less likely than strong Republicans to voluntarily read a "surprising climate-skeptical story," whereas a "surprising climate-concerned story" was far more likely to be read by those on the left than on the right. One encouraging mitigating factor was "science curiosity," or the "motivation to seek out and consume scientific information for personal pleasure," which "seems to counteract rather than aggravate the signature characteristics of politically motivated reasoning."

The authors concluded that "individuals who have an appetite to be *surprised* by scientific information—who find it pleasurable to discover that the world does not work as they expected—do not turn this feature of their personality *off* when they engage political information but rather indulge it in that setting as well, exposing themselves more readily to information that defies their expectations about facts on contested issues. The result is that these citizens, unlike their less curious counterparts, react more open-mindedly and respond more uniformly across the political spectrum to the best available evidence."

In other words, valuing science for pure pleasure is more of a bulwark against the politicization of science than facts alone.

About the Author

Michael Shermer is publisher of Skeptic *magazine and a Presidential Fellow at Chapman University. His latest book is* Heavens on Earth: The Scientific Search for the Afterlife, Immortality, and Utopia *(Henry Holt, 2018).*

Denial of Evolution Is a Form of White Supremacy

By Allison Hopper

After a year of lockdown, museums, libraries and bookstores across America are reopening. This cultural reawakening's beginning coincided with both the Juneteenth holiday and the one-year anniversary of the one of the largest protests in American history against racial injustice. As bookstores reopen, many are organizing displays of children's books that celebrate Black history. What you won't find in even the biggest collections of books is the story of the dark-skinned early people who launched human civilization.

The global scientific community overwhelmingly accepts that all living humans are of African descent. Most scientific articles about our African origins focus on genetics. The part of the story that is not widely shared is about the creation of human culture. We are all descended genetically, and also culturally, from dark-skinned ancestors. Early humans from the African continent are the ones who first invented tools; the use of fire; language; and religion. These dark skinned early people laid down the foundation for human culture. Considering the short life span of our early ancestors, these original innovators were probably also very young. No one who follows artistic trends will be surprised to learn that, from the beginning, human culture was essentially invented by teenagers. And by culture I don't just mean the arts, I mean the whole shebang.

I want to unmask the lie that evolution denial is about religion and recognize that at its core, it is a form of white supremacy that perpetuates segregation and violence against Black bodies. Under the guise of "religious freedom," the legalistic wing of creationists loudly insists that their point of view deserves equal time in the classroom. Science education in the U.S. is constantly on the defensive against anti-evolution activists who want biblical stories to be taught as fact.

In fact, the first wave of legal fights against evolution was supported by the Klan in the 1920s. Ever since then, entrenched racism and the ban on teaching evolution in the schools have gone hand in hand. In his piece, *What We Get Wrong About the Evolution Debate*, Adam Shapiro argues that "the history of American controversies over evolution has long been entangled with the history of American educational racism."

At the heart of white evangelical creationism is the mythology of an unbroken white lineage that stretches back to a light-skinned Adam and Eve. In literal interpretations of the Christian Bible, white skin was created in God's image. Dark skin has a different, more problematic origin. As the biblical story goes, the curse or mark of Cain for killing his brother was a darkening of his descendants' skin. Historically, many congregations in the U.S. pointed to this story of Cain as evidence that Black skin was created as a punishment.

The fantasy of a continuous line of white descendants segregates white heritage from Black bodies. In the real world, this mythology translates into lethal effects on people who are Black. Fundamentalist interpretations of the Bible are part of the "fake news" epidemic that feeds the racial divide in our country.

For too long, a vocal minority of creationists has hijacked children's education, media and book publishing. Statistics on creationist beliefs in the U.S. vary. Depending on the poll, up to 40 percent of percent of adults believe that humans have always existed in their present form (i.e., they believe in an unbroken human lineage stretching back to Adam and Eve).

We have seen some progress in the classroom. From 2007 to 2019, the percentage of teachers who present evolution without a creationist alternative grew dramatically, from only 51 percent to 67 percent. But it's still not enough. My hope is that if we make the connection between creationism and racist ideology clearer, we will provide more ammunition to get science into the classroom—and into our culture at large.

It's common knowledge that some school boards, especially in the South, have fought long and hard to keep evolution out of school textbooks. What you might not know is how the policing of educational content morphs into what might be called "self-censorship" within the children's book industry as a whole. Scientific findings about human origins have been slow to trickle down into books written for young people. This major omission reflects the outsize effect that science-denying voices have on the books that find their ways not just into classrooms, but also into libraries, bookstores and children's homes. Fear of economic punishment within the publishing industry creates a self-perpetuating lack of teaching materials about evolution.

If you go on Amazon and look up "children's books on evolution" you will find about 10-15 relevant titles. This is in contrast to the hundreds of children's books on other scientific subjects such as chemistry, astronomy and other less controversial subjects. I found only one book on evolution for preschoolers, called *Grandmother Fish*. The author had to self-fund the book through Kickstarter.

On the other hand, there are hundreds of children's books available on Amazon that focus on biblical origin stories. Science deniers are pumping money into a well-funded anti-evolution machine. In 2007, the creationists built their own Bible-themed museum and amusement park. What they understand is that to reach young children you need music, colorful characters and celebration.

In the Adam-and-Eve scenario, the Creator bestows both physical and cultural humanity on the first people. From the get-go Adam knows how to name the animals. No one has to invent language or figure out how to make tools. Science, of course, tells us otherwise. The process of natural selection shaped our bodies and capacities. Our humanity emerged over the millennia as creative ancient people figured out the crucial skills–from storytelling to cooking to rope making–that we now take for granted.

And yet, even in the current literature about human origins that we do have, the end point of evolution is often depicted as a white man carrying a spear. This image not only eliminates our African heritage but also erases women and children from the picture.

Because evolution is foundational knowledge, we need the story to be told in many different ways, by many different voices.

As we move forward to undo systemic racism in every aspect of business, society, academia and life, let's be sure to do so in science education as well. Embracing humanity's dark-skinned ancestors with love and respect is key to changing our relationship to the past, and to creating racial equity in the present. These ancient people made the rest of us possible. Opening our hearts to them and embracing them as heroic, fully human and worthy of our respect is part of the process of healing from our racist history.

This is an opinion and analysis article; the views expressed by the author or authors are not necessarily those of Scientific American.

About the Author

Allison Hopper is a filmmaker and designer with a master's degree in educational design from New York University. Early in her career, she worked on PBS documentaries. More recently, she's been creating content for young people on the topic of evolution. She has presented on evolution at the Big History Conference in Amsterdam and Chautauqua, among other places.

Scientists Should Admit They Bring Personal Values to Their Work

By Naomi Oreskes

As the U.S. recoils from the divisions of recent years and the scientific community tries to rebuild trust in science, scientists may be tempted to reaffirm their neutrality. If people are to trust us again, as I have frequently heard colleagues argue, we have to be scrupulous about not allowing our values to intrude into our science. This presupposes that value neutrality is necessary for public trust and that it is possible. But available evidence suggests that neither presumption is correct.

Recent research in communications has shown that people are most likely to accept a message when it is delivered by trusted messengers–teachers, for example, or religious or business leaders, or local doctors and nurses. One strategy to build trust, therefore, is for scientists to build links from their laboratories, institutes and academic departments into the communities where they live and work. One way to do this is by partnering with organizations such as the National Center for Science Education, founded to fight creationism in the classroom but now working broadly with teachers to increase understanding of the nature of science itself. To do this, scientists do not need to throw off their personal values; they merely need to share with teachers a belief in the value of education. This is important because research suggests that, even if we try, we can't throw off our values.

It is well known that people are more likely to accept evidence that accords with what they already believe. Psychologists call this "motivated reasoning," and although the term is relatively recent, the insight is not. Four hundred years ago Francis Bacon put it this way: "Human understanding is not composed of dry light, but is subject to influence from the will and the emotions ... man prefers to believe what he wants to be true."

Scientists may assume this motivated reasoning explains erroneous positions—such as the refusal to wear a mask to limit the spread of COVID-19—but plays little role in science. Alas, there is little evidence to support such confidence. Some research suggests that even with financial incentives, most people are apparently incapable of escaping their biases. Thus, the problem seems to be not a matter of *will* but of capacity. Great scientists may think because they are trained to be objective, they can avoid the pitfalls into which ordinary people fall. But that isn't necessarily the case.

Does this mean that science cannot be objective? No. What makes it so is not scientists patrolling their own biases but rather the mechanisms used to ensure that bias is minimized. Peer review is the best known of these, though equally if not more important is diversity. As I contend in the new edition of my book *Why Trust Science?*, diversity in science is crucial not just to ensure that every person has a chance to develop their talent but to ensure that science is as unbiased as possible.

Some will argue that value neutrality is an ideal toward which we should strive, even if we know it can't be achieved entirely. In the practice of science, this argument may hold. But what is useful in scientific research may be counterproductive in public communication because the idea of a trusted messenger implies shared values. Studies show that U.S. scientists want (among other things) to use their knowledge to improve health, make life easier, strengthen the economy through innovation and discovery, and protect people from losses associated with disruptive climate change.

Opinion polls suggest that most Americans want many of these things, too; 73 percent of us believe that science has a mostly positive impact on society. If scientists decline to discuss their values for fear that they conflict with the values of their audiences, they may miss the opportunity to discover significant points of overlap and agreement. If, on the other hand, scientists insist on their value neutrality, they will likely come across as inauthentic, if not dishonest. A person who truly had no values—or refused to allow values to influence their decision-making—would be a sociopath!

Value neutrality is a tinfoil shield. Rather than trying to hide behind it, scientists should admit that they have values and be proud that these values motivate research aiming to make the world a better place for all.

About the Author

Naomi Oreskes is a professor of the history of science at Harvard University. She is author of Why Trust Science? *(Princeton University Press, 2019) and co-author of* Discerning Experts *(University of Chicago, 2019).*

Section 2: Evolution in the Classroom

2.1 50 Years Ago: Repeal of Tennessee's "Monkey Law"
By Glenn Branch and Ann Reid

2.2 Dissent with Modification: Soothing Evolution-Religion Tensions in the Classroom
By Robin Lloyd

2.3 Teachers Help One Another Bring Evolution Back to the Classroom
By Adam Piore

2.4 Evolution Is Still True, but...
By Glenn Branch

2.5 Evolution Education in the U.S. Is Getting Better
By Glenn Branch and Ann Reid

2.6 Science Education Is Under Legislative Attack
By Glenn Branch and Mano Singham

50 Years Ago: Repeal of Tennessee's "Monkey Law"

By Glenn Branch and Ann Reid

Gary Scott hadn't realized that he wasn't supposed to teach evolution. But on April 13, 1967, the young Jacksboro, Tenn., science teacher was fired for violating section 49-1922 of the Tennessee Code–the so-called Butler Act, also known as the "Monkey Law," under which a different young science teacher in Tennessee was indicted, prosecuted and convicted 42 years earlier, in *The State of Tennessee v. John Thomas Scopes*. Thanks in part to a legal challenge filed by Scott to the constitutionality of the Butler Act, the Tennessee legislature decided to repeal the law, and the governor signed the repeal measure on May 18, 1967. Shortly thereafter, the remaining state bans on the teaching of evolution–in Arkansas and Mississippi–were ruled to be unconstitutional in the courts.

Half a century later, though, the schools are still not entirely safe for evolution.

From Scopes through Scott to today, science teachers have been in the trenches of the evolution wars, bearing the brunt of conflicting forces from science and society. In science, evolution is universally accepted on the basis of overwhelming evidence from diverse lines of inquiry. In society, however, it is often regarded with suspicion, arising mainly from a view that evolution conflicts with the creation accounts of the Bible.

The magnitude of the disconnection between science and society is suggested by a survey conducted by the Pew Research Center in 2014, according to which 98 percent of American scientists accepted evolution, but only 62 percent of the American general public agreed, with 34 percent preferring a creationist alternative–"Humans have existed in their present form since the beginning of time"–instead.

Not all of those 31 percent vehemently deny evolution, to be sure. Surveys that allow respondents to indicate their level of confidence in their answers or that add "don't know" and "not sure" as possible answers reveal substantial ambivalence and uncertainty in public opinion on evolution, with relatively few ardent creationists. But in a climate of doubt, denial is able to exert disproportionate influence.

Prompted by fundamentalist religious attitudes, doubt and denial about evolution motivated the passage of the Butler Act in Tennessee in 1925. They have not disappeared in the 50 years since its repeal. The strategies used to launch attacks on the teaching of evolution in the public schools have mutated, however, striving to adapt to shifting legal, political and educational landscapes.

When banning the teaching of evolution failed as a strategy, evolution's opponents were forced to take a different approach: calling for the teaching of a supposed alternative to evolution for the sake of balance. The alternatives–biblical creationism, creation science, intelligent design–were advanced with increasingly determined attempts to conceal their religious basis in the hope that they would survive the scrutiny of the courts.

But these alternatives were found to be unconstitutional at every turn. A Tennessee state law requiring textbooks to include biblical creationism was struck down in 1975; Arkansas and Louisiana state laws requiring balancing evolution with creation science were struck down in 1982 and 1987; and a Pennsylvania school district's policy requiring the presentation of intelligent design was struck down in 2005.

Even before the legal defeat of intelligent design in Pennsylvania, evolution's opponents were already beginning to try yet a different tack: requiring, or more commonly allowing, science teachers to misrepresent evolution as scientifically controversial, often under the rubric of academic freedom. More than 70 such bills have been introduced since 2004, with three enacted, in Mississippi, Louisiana and Tennessee.

It is unclear to what extent science teachers in those three states take advantage of those laws. But according to a national survey conducted in 2007, about one in eight public high school biology teachers present creationism as scientifically credible in their classrooms, despite the unconstitutionality of the practice.

Scientific, educational and legal concerns are often overridden by personal or community attitudes of doubt and denial.

Indeed, the same survey revealed that six in 10 of the instructors were teaching evolution less than forthrightly–compromising on the accuracy, completeness or rigor of their treatment, often for fear of provoking a creationist backlash. Such fears, sadly, appear to be warranted: more than one in five of the teachers reported experiencing community resistance to their teaching of evolution.

Fortunately, the treatment of evolution in state science standards is getting better on the whole, which means that textbooks, curricula and, ideally, teachers are following suit. But scientific knowledge and pedagogical know-how are not the only equipment that educators need to teach evolution. They also need the confidence to persist, even in the face of doubt and denial.

Creationists are as active as ever, with a few even in the bully pulpits afforded by high political office. And the legal rulings that established the obstacles that have so far thwarted attacks on evolution education could be overturned by a reactionary Supreme Court or circumvented by public support of religious schools not subject to constitutional strictures. So the evolution wars are by no means over.

Gary Scott's own service in the evolution wars was for just a brief skirmish: he was reinstated–with back pay–at Jacksboro High School even before the Butler Act was repealed. He wasn't the last science teacher to play the role of hero in the contentious history of evolution education in the U.S. But science teachers shouldn't have to engage in heroics to present evolution forthrightly, without fear and beyond reproach.

The views expressed are those of the author(s) and are not necessarily those of Scientific American.

About the Authors

Glenn Branch is deputy director and Ann Reid is executive director of the National Center for Science Education, a nonprofit organization that supports the accurate teaching of evolution and climate change.

Dissent with Modification: Soothing Evolution–Religion Tensions in the Classroom

By Robin Lloyd

On topics ranging from astrophysics to public health, rejections of scientific consensus can prove quite inflexible when bolstered by religious doctrine. But a new approach to teaching evolutionary biology appears to ease such tensions. It involves airing perceived conflicts between religion and evolution in the classroom rather than simply presenting a mountain of evidence for evolution. Such a curriculum could help biologists (most of whom claim to hold no religious beliefs) more effectively prepare students (most of whom profess belief in God) to meet the nation's growing need for scientists and technologists.

During a two-week module on evolution that was part of an introductory biology course at Arizona State University, the instructor explored a variety of viewpoints about the relation between some religious beliefs and the development and diversification of life, ranging from evolution without the involvement of a deity to various types of creationism–including theistic evolution. Students were encouraged to express their opinions and concerns.

Surveys filled out by 60 students before and after the module revealed that the number of students who perceived a sense of a conflict between religion and evolution at the start was cut in half by the end. An analysis of the results is detailed in the February 2017 issue of the *American Biology Teacher*.

In response to instructors' concerns about limited classroom time, a follow-up project compressed the two-week module to six minutes. Remarkably, unpublished results suggest this brief exposure also proved effective at reducing students' perception of a conflict. "If we encourage national policy documents that promote these teaching practices," says study co-author Elizabeth Barnes of Arizona

State, "perhaps we can increase acceptance of evolution among our students, future teachers and future political leaders."

About the Author

Journalist Robin Lloyd, a contributing editor at Scientific American, *is president of the Council for the Advancement of Science Writing's board of directors.*

Teachers Help One Another Bring Evolution Back to the Classroom

By Adam Piore

Patti Howell had thought long and hard about this moment in her 10th-grade biology class. She had spent months subtly preparing her students for it, had agonized and worried about it, had even attended a training session to get ready for it.

Now, on a sun-dappled April morning, Howell stood before 26 15-year-olds at the Baconton Community Charter School in southwestern Georgia, scanning the slip of paper she had just plucked off a heavy wood table.

"All right, let's see what we got here," said Howell, a 40-something teacher, wearing horn-rimmed glasses and a loose floral print shirt. "Biologists 'believe' in evolution. How many of you think that is fact?"

Hands shot up around the classroom, along with a chorus of "fact," spoken in adolescent murmurs.

"Majority are saying fact," Howell said.

She nodded sagely–she had set up perfectly the exercise she learned in her training session. Now it was time for the payoff.

"Science is not a belief system," she said. "Science is a collection of evidence, reporting and communicating what you get from that evidence. You do not 'believe' in evolution; you do not 'believe' in science."

Howell scanned her students' faces.

"Religion is our belief system," she continued. "I believe in God, I have faith in God, I do not need for God to burn a bush in front of me. But for science we need evidence."

It's day one of the evolution unit in Howell's class. And for a science teacher, the job doesn't get much more challenging than this. Baconton, population 850, is a devout farming community known for growing easy-to-crack pecans. A road sign at the entrance to town welcomes visitors to "the paper shell pecan capital of the world." Almost all Howell's students attend local Baptist congregations that follow a "strict literalist" interpretation of the Bible. Their pastors teach that God created Earth in six 24-hour days, including Adam and Eve, and that humans do not share a common ancestor with lower life-forms. Most of Howell's colleagues have strong beliefs on the topic, too. When the Spanish teacher in the classroom across the hall learned that evolution was on today's agenda, he asked Howell for the names of her 50 students. He wanted to pray for their souls.

Howell thinks what she is doing right now, as she begins the evolution unit, is key to everything that will follow. Somehow she must convince her students that they can consider what she has to say about evolution with an open mind and still retain the religious beliefs that lie at the center of their cultural identity—that, contrary to what many of their pastors tell them every Sunday, she is not attempting to force them to choose between God and science.

It's a tough sell. Which is why, for months, Howell has refused to discuss the subject with her students. Many had been asking her from the first day of school: Do you believe in evolution? Do you think we came from monkeys?

Now Howell looks out at the faces of her students and finally answers.

"I know that y'all think I'm a heathen," she says. "I understand that, but I am Christian. Do I believe in evolution? No, that's not a belief system. But I accept the theory of evolution."

Avoiding the Subject

Straight talk about evolution in classrooms is less common than one might think. According to the most comprehensive study of public school biology teachers, just 28 percent implement the major recommendations and conclusions of the National Research Council, which call for them to "unabashedly introduce evidence that evolution has occurred and craft lesson plans so that evolution is a theme that unifies disparate topics in biology," according to a 2011 *Science* article by Pennsylvania State University political scientists Michael Berkman and Eric Plutzer.

Conversely, 13 percent of teachers (found in virtually every state in the Union and the District of Columbia) reported explicitly advocating creationism or intelligent design by spending at least an hour of class time presenting it in a positive light. Another 5 percent said they endorsed creationism in passing while answering student questions.

The majority—60 percent of teachers—either attempted to avoid the topic of evolution altogether, quickly blew past it, allowing students to debate evolution, or "watered down" their lessons, Plutzer says. Many said they feared the reaction of students, parents and religious members of their community. And although only 2 percent of teachers reported avoiding the topic entirely, 17 percent, or roughly one in six teachers, avoided discussing human evolution. Many others simply raced through it.

To confront these challenges, several organizations have launched new kinds of training sessions that are aimed at better preparing teachers for what they will face in the classroom. Moreover, a growing number of researchers have begun to examine the causes of these teaching failures and new ways to overcome them.

Among many educators, a new idea has begun to take root: perhaps it is time to rethink the way evolution teachers grapple with religion (or choose not to grapple with it) in the classroom. "There has been this war between creationism and what I think of as a cold teaching of evolution. Basically, 'Check your religious beliefs at the door, we don't talk about that in here, this is science. All you narrow-minded fundamentalist Christians, shut up and listen to us talk,'" says Lee Meadows, an associate professor of science education at the University of Alabama at Birmingham. Meadows also serves on the social impact committee of the Smithsonian Institution's Human Origins Initiative, a group helping to find ways to better promote acceptance of evolution education. "There's a growing number of us," he adds, "who are saying there's got to be a way to teach the science without throwing kids who come from religious backgrounds into turmoil."

A Legacy of Acrimony

For decades the most high-stakes, high-profile battles over evolution education were fought in the courts and state legislatures. The debate centered on, among other things, whether the subject itself could be banned or whether lawmakers could require that equal time be given to the biblical account of creation or the idea of "intelligent design." Now, with those questions largely resolved—courts have overwhelmingly sided with those pushing to keep evolution in the classroom and creationism out of it—the battle lines have moved into the schools themselves.

The most promising efforts nowadays are focused on laws advocating "academic freedom," which leave it up to individual teachers to say what they want about controversial science topics, including evolution, says Glenn Branch, deputy director of the National Center for Science Education, which monitors anti-science legislation.

"If you can't ban the teaching of evolution, and you can't balance it with creationism in some form or other, what do you do?" Branch asks. "You belittle it, you say evolution is just a theory or you say it's controversial. Creationists have been saying this all along. The difference is that now they don't have anything better."

Today, many are now realizing, the far larger obstacle for the vast majority of ordinary science teachers is the legacy of acrimony left over from the decades of legal battles. In many communities, evolution education remains so charged with controversy that teachers either water down their lesson plans, devote as little time as possible to the subject or attempt to avoid it altogether.

Meanwhile teachers in deeply religious communities such as Baconton face an additional challenge. Often they lack tools and methods that allow them to teach evolution in a way that does not force those students to take sides—a choice that usually does not go well for the scientists perceived to be at war with their community.

Without such tools, even those teachers who do feel confident with the material often have trouble convincing students to listen to their lesson plans with an open mind—or to listen to them at all.

From the Courtroom to the Classroom

The war over evolution education has had three distinct phases leading up to the current era, according to NCSE's Branch.

The first wave of anti-evolution pressure in public schools started in the 1920s, when a number of states attempted to ban the teaching of evolution outright. After conspiring with a local businessman, a young substitute teacher in Tennessee named John T. Scopes deliberately defied the ban, taught evolution, and was arrested and charged with a misdemeanor. The intent was always to challenge his arrest in court. His trial, which began in July 1925, led to a spectacular showdown between defense attorney Clarence Darrow and prosecutor William Jennings Bryan, was broadcast on radio and transfixed the nation. Scopes was convicted, but the conviction was later overturned on a technicality, allowing proponents of the ban to avoid a ruling on its constitutionality that many had by then determined they were very likely to lose.

The ban was not actually overturned on constitutional grounds until 1968, when a similar Arkansas law was overturned by the U.S. Supreme Court in *Epperson v. Arkansas*. After that, anti-evolution forces moved to a second approach: advocating the teaching of creationism alongside evolution.

In the 1975 Tennessee case *Daniel v. Waters*, courts struck down an "equal time" law passed by the state legislature, requiring teachers to teach biblical creation whenever they taught evolution. Throughout the 1970s and 1980s, Branch notes, some 30 state legislatures considered bills advocating the teaching of "creation science," arguing that creation accounts of genesis, including the worldwide flood, were scientifically supportable.

A bill in Arkansas actually passed, leading to its defeat in the 1982 case *McLean v. Arkansas*, which featured evolutionary biologist Stephen Jay Gould and a whole host of celebrity scientists. Soon after, Louisiana passed a broader bill, which was struck down by the Supreme Court in 1987.

After those defeats, many moved on to advocating the teaching of intelligent design, which argues that "something, somehow, intervened in the history of life," according to Branch. That approach was struck down in 2005 by a federal district judge, after parents in Dover, Pa., challenged a policy put in place by a local school board that had been taken over by creationists (who were subsequently voted out).

In the minds of many, that put a stop to any credible legislative effort to bring creationism back to the classroom. Yet the issue hasn't gone away. No one knows that better than teachers on the front lines such as Patti Howell.

On the first day of the evolution unit, Howell set to work subtly chipping away at her students' resistance to the theory. As soon as her backpack-toting teenagers shuffled past her that morning, she handed each one a brief article on the evolutionary vulnerability of asexually reproducing toenail fungus. Then she instructed them to partner up and rotate through a series of stations set up around the room.

As she had done with her two other biology classes, at each station she had placed a slip of paper with a single statement on it: "Humans evolved from monkeys," read one. "Only Atheists accept the theory of evolution," read another. After reading each slip, the students placed beads on one of two sticks, each anchored by a small wood square labeled either "fact" or "fiction." Howell addressed the "misconceptions" one by one. Then she played brief video clips about dog fleas that have developed resistance to store-bought anti-itch creams and bacteria that have grown resistant to antibiotics.

Her goals on this first day were twofold: to provide examples of evolution that students might observe every day and to address common misconceptions.

Howell learned these two approaches at a recent teacher-training session sponsored by the Teacher Institute for Evolutionary Science (TIES), an organization launched in 2015 by Miami-Dade middle school teacher Bertha Vazquez, with funding from the Richard Dawkins Foundation for Reason and Science. During the past three years TIES has held 92 workshops in more than 30 states and trained upward of 1,500 teachers. Countless others have accessed the organization's webinars remotely.

The idea, Vazquez says, is to take aim at perhaps the biggest obstacle to evolution education: the fact that many teachers feel unprepared to teach it. "If I mess up when I'm teaching weather to my students—say I don't know the difference between an occluded front and a stationary front—no one is calling the office and nobody's really going to question me," Vazquez explains. "If I mess up between natural selection and genetic drift or theory versus fact, then you're going to have parents on you full of misconceptions. If you don't feel confident teaching this, you're just not going to teach it."

In 2013 Vazquez participated in a discussion with Richard Dawkins and about a dozen science professors at the University of Miami about exactly this issue. They concluded the problem is that teachers are not comfortable with the material. Therefore, after the event, she set up a professional development course in evolution for some of her friends in area middle schools. When Vazquez met Dawkins a year later at another event and told him what she had done, Dawkins offered to come talk to her teachers. And a few months later Dawkins asked if Vazquez might be willing to take her project national. (Dawkins serves on *Scientific American*'s board of advisers.)

In 2016 the program added webinars, available to teachers who cannot make it to the workshops in person. These resources supplement a growing body of teaching materials already on the Web—in 2004, for instance, the National Center for Science Education, in collaboration with the University of California Museum of Paleontology, developed a Web site entitled Understanding Evolution that offers science content, teaching resources and teaching strategies. "We're trying to get teachers to a point where they have confidence teaching it and can present it for what it is," Vazquez says, "a beautiful awe-inspiring way of seeing the world, you know, that's current and relevant."

Although Vazquez, who teaches in a Miami-Dade school, does not face nearly the level of resistance Howell is confronting, she estimates every year she has a handful of students for whom evolution is a problem, either Christians, Muslims or Jehovah's Witnesses. And when designing her training materials, she built in the approaches she has found to be effective and intuitive in engaging them.

"If you start with misconceptions, and modern, current relevance of evolution and how important it is in terms of agriculture and medicine, it brings their guard down a little bit," Vazquez says. "I think showing just a common little example, those kids can go home now and say, 'yeah, she talked about fleas.' The teacher's not really going to get in trouble, but the kids are going to get natural selection."

"When teachers ask us about how to deal with students' religious questions in TIES workshops, we recommend the teachers say, 'Since this is a science class, we will not address religion here. We advise you to ask your parents and faith leaders about the religious question,'" Vazquez adds. Howell herself chose to add in a mention of her own religious beliefs to drive home the idea that religion and science coexist.

The approaches that Vazquez and Howell have arrived at through intuition and experience, others are confirming or refining using the scientific method. Indeed, a growing number of researchers are beginning to argue that in addition to tackling misconceptions and showing evolution at work in the world today, it may actually be equally effective to explicitly address the elephant in the science room: religion.

In one influential 2011 study published in the *Journal of Research in Science Teaching*, investigators at Southern Nazarene University, Purdue University and Florida State University examined the experiences of 15 biology majors at a Midwestern Christian university who were raised to believe in creationism but were forced to grapple with evolution. In the end, almost all of them came to accept evolution. The researchers wanted to know why. In fact, rather than glossing over religion, they found, their professors had acknowledged the religious beliefs of their students, talked openly about the issues raised and served as role models who could help the students reconcile the science with their beliefs.

In another 2012 study, a researcher at Towson University explored the difference between religious students who were unwilling to learn evolution and those who were able to learn and understand evolution, despite the fact that they did not believe in it. In that study, researchers suggested, among other things, that when teachers failed to mention religion it increased their feelings of alienation and made them less open to learning.

Inspired by this research, Arizona State University researchers Sara Brownell and Elizabeth Barnes set out to find out how often professors actually did approach evolution in the college classroom. Not only did they find that instructors rarely touch on the issue of religion, they found the likely reason. The vast majority of instructors teaching evolution were atheists, whereas the population of students who identify as religious in the class was sometimes as high as 80 percent. "When we asked the professors why, they often cited reasons that were related to their own religious cultural background," Barnes says. "Mainly that they didn't have experience talking about these issues, and so it was a little intimidating. They weren't aware of their students' religious beliefs and whether their students were struggling with evolution. And they had some negative stereotypes."

Yet to those who grew up in devoutly religious communities and have gone through the process of learning evolution, it is obvious that ignoring religion won't work. Amanda Glaze, who is a professor of middle grades and secondary education at Georgia Southern University, was inspired to study evolution education in part by her own experience. After growing up in a creationist family on an

Alabama farm, she fell in love with science and eventually came to accept Darwin's theory of evolution. But it was not an easy journey.

"I cried, I was depressed, I was worried that I was going to Hell. I mean, years, years of literal torment back and forth," she recalls. "And yet we try to come into a classroom in a semester or a year and tell people, 'Oh, well, you know, your beliefs are wrong,' or 'They don't matter, this is what's true.' And people wonder why evolutionary acceptance in this country is abysmal." What many evolution education advocates do not realize, Glaze says, is that for many, religious beliefs and worldviews are "an identity construct." "If you're not a part of that, if you've never experienced that, it's very easy to say well, it doesn't matter, you're just being irrational," she says. "Students will just shut down."

To reconcile her new knowledge with her identity, Glaze says, required her to find a way to consciously segregate her religious beliefs from her scientific knowledge and let them each exist independently, an approach process some have termed "cognitive apartheid." "We have science, which is a physical explanation of events occurring in a physical world, then we have religious ways of knowing, philosophical ways of knowing that are not tied to physical evidence," Glaze says. "The standards and the burdens in those different ways of knowing are very, very starkly different, but so often we try to conflate the two."

"It's not a matter of supplanting or breaking down someone's existing worldview. What our actual goal should be is to add a scientific worldview to whatever worldviews people are bringing to the classroom. But to do that, you have to recognize what those worldviews are and the power that they hold with people."

David Wilcox, a professor emeritus of biology at Eastern University, a Baptist school located in Pennsylvania, spent more than 35 years teaching evolution to students who came in believing in creationism. And for him, "disentangling" the messages received about religion and science was essential. "What's happened is that evolution is taught in an awful lot of churches not as a matter of science but as a part of a worldview packaged with other ideas–including the idea that one does not believe in God and a worldview in which morality will disappear and in which civilization is not going to survive," he says. "Many of my students come in having been taught that if you believe in evolution, you have to believe all those other things are true, too. But that's not the case."

Wilcox was consistently successful with his students because the first thing he did was attempt to break apart these disparate ideas and convince his students that it is possible to deal with science and still have faith. He also emphasized that there are theologians who have interpretations of the Bible different from those of strict literalists (St. Augustine, for instance)–that, in fact, the theological interpretations that God created Earth in six "literal" days is not at all universal. At the very least, he shows them there is "another door" they can return to later that leads to acceptance of evolution that does not come with atheism.

Finding Religion

Perhaps the most promising and potentially impactful resource to address religion and evolution in the classroom is being developed by Briana Pobiner, a prehistoric archaeologist and museum educator at the Smithsonian Institution's National Museum of Natural History, and her colleagues in close consultation with educational researchers and faith leaders who meet several times a year through the Smithsonian's Human Origins Initiative's social impact committee. Recently they unveiled a 75-page *Cultural and Religious Sensitivity (CRS) Teaching Strategies Resource* guide for teachers to use for discussing human evolution and for actively testing their techniques in the classroom.

"Ignoring the issue of religion doesn't work," Pobiner says. "But there is a way to engage students' faith perspective and help them not shut down completely. Increasingly we are finding that when you don't dismiss students' faith perspective, you get a much better outcome for helping them engage with the content of evolution."

Among other things, the document includes several classroom exercises that teachers can introduce either at the start of evolutionary instruction or "at the first signs of unexpected negativity"—"not to change personal or cultural religious beliefs or to resolve any conflicts between science and religion your students may feel, but to help your student understand the nature of science and that the theory of evolution is a scientific tool useful in addressing biological questions."

In the first exercise, students are given a homework assignment that asks them to summarize the theory of evolution, to summarize alternative explanations for the variety of life-forms that are important to people they know and to list reasons why some people might be concerned about the study of evolution. In class, the students then break up into groups to discuss their answers.

Over the course of the 2012–2013 school year, Pobiner and her colleagues field-tested the CRS materials with AP biology students in 10 schools in eight states. They used assessments of students' understanding of evolution before and after it was taught to test their effectiveness. In results published earlier this year in the journal *Evolution: Education and Outreach*, Pobiner and her colleagues found that students who had done the CRS exercise had a better understanding and acceptance of the theory of evolution.

The group is now testing this approach in a more challenging environment: 9th-grade biology classes across Alabama, the only state in the union where biology textbooks bear a sticker warning that evolution is "just a theory" and should not be taken as fact. (Alabama lawmakers also passed a resolution last year affirming teachers' rights to include creationism in their lesson plans.)

Birmingham's Meadows says the findings will be presented at the Alabama teachers association in November. "Alabama teachers are wanting permission to teach evolution, and they want to know they can do it without personal turmoil and student turmoil, and that's what I think we're going to show," Meadows notes. "It's going to be huge." No studies have yet been done on the TIES approach.

Chipping Away at Resistance

Every Sunday, Patti Howell sits in a pew of her church in the town of Americus and listens to her preacher preach: Those scientists are going to try and tell you this. Those scientists are going to try and tell you that.

She never broaches the topic of evolution with her friends, and on the few times she and her husband have discussed the matter, they have argued.

"In church, I just keep my mouth shut. I would never open my mouth. I don't discuss it with my friends and family," she says. "I just sit there and listen to it."

Howell doesn't have that option in her class–she has a job to do. And she knows the hardest part lies ahead.

Accepting the biological resistance of bacteria is one thing. She expects many of her students will even be interested in the adaptations Darwin discovered in the beak shapes of finches separated from their ancestors by geography. The problems, she expects, will begin when she gets to the similarities between humans and other species–commonalities in DNA, vestigial structures such as the tailbone and other evidence that humans share common ancestors with other species. This part of evolution, she knows, is hard to reconcile with the biblical accounts of creation, Adam and Eve, and the Garden of Eden. "They're going to have a hard time with that," she says.

Howell has had enough experience teaching evolution in other communities for 17 years to know the signs. The students will cross their arms; they will stare at the floor. The most defiant among them may even kick the chairs on the way out. Although she believes the tools she has learned through the TIES program will improve her chances of reaching some students, she knows she won't reach them all.

Howell isn't sure what kind of class she will have in coming years. She is hungry for more tools to help her navigate the cultural minefield in her classroom. It's a lonely battle but one she is willing to fight. "I've got these people's kids, and that's the most important thing in the whole world to anybody," she says. "I don't want to tell them something wrong or damage them. It's a huge responsibility."

Referenced

Defeating Creationism in the Courtroom, but Not in the Classroom. Michael B. Berkman and Eric Plutzer in *Science*, Vol. 331, pages 404–405; January 28, 2011.

Evolution Education in the American South: Culture, Politics, and Resources in and around Alabama. Edited by Christopher D. Lynn, Amanda L. Glaze, William A. Evans and Laura K. Reed. Palgrave Macmillan, 2017.

Using Human Case Studies to Teach Evolution in High School A.P. Biology Classrooms. Briana Pobiner, Paul M. Beardsley, Constance M. Bertka and William A. Watson in *Evolution: Education and Outreach*, Vol. 11, No. 1, Article No. 3; December 2018.

About the Author

Adam Piore is a freelance journalist. His last article for Scientific American *examined the movement to bring evolution back to the classroom.*

Evolution Is Still True, but ...

By Glenn Branch

November 12, 2018, was a date worth celebrating. It was the 50th anniversary of the Supreme Court's decision in *Epperson v. Arkansas*, which struck down a state law prohibiting the teaching of evolution in Arkansas's public schools. In his opinion for the court, Justice Abe Fortas wrote, "there can be no doubt that Arkansas has sought to prevent its teachers from discussing the theory of evolution because it is contrary to the belief of some that the Book of Genesis must be the exclusive doctrine as to the origin of man," finding the law in violation of the First Amendment's Establishment Clause.

In the wake of the Epperson decision, anti-evolution campaigners regrouped with efforts to "balance" the teaching of evolution in the public schools with various supposedly scientifically credible alternatives: biblical creation, creation science and intelligent design. None of these efforts survived constitutional scrutiny, with these various forms of creationism defeated in such cases as *Daniel v. Waters* (1975), *McLean v. Arkansas* (1982), *Edwards v. Aguillard* (1987) and *Kitzmiller v. Dover* (2005)–all citing the Epperson decision as a crucial precedent.

That's why the preferred strategy is now to belittle evolution, while remaining silent about any supposed alternatives. In Arizona, for example, although the superintendent of public instruction favors teaching intelligent design alongside evolution in public school science classrooms, she refrained from inserting intelligent design in a new set of state science education standards. Instead, she arranged for the treatment of evolution to be downplayed, even recently appointing a creation science advocate to a committee charged with revising the portions of the standards addressing evolution.

Why is it important for state science standards to present evolution properly? Partly to encourage teachers themselves. Sadly, evolution remains socially controversial. Indeed, in a rigorous national survey of public high school biology teachers conducted in 2007, more than one in four of the respondents reported experiencing pressure to downplay evolution. The more accurate, complete and forthright the treatment of evolution is in their state science standards, the easier it is for these teachers to teach evolution properly, even in the face of such pressure.

The benefits of a set of state science standards with a good treatment of evolution aren't confined to beleaguered science teachers. State science standards provide guidelines for local school districts to follow in developing their science curricula. They determine the content of statewide science examinations. They are consulted by textbook publishers while developing their biology textbooks. And they set the agenda for the training of teachers, both in their own education and in their professional development. So, the content of state science standards makes a crucial difference.

A good set of state science standards isn't going to be the only ally of teachers who want to teach evolution properly. With 99 percent of active research scientists accepting evolution and a host of scientific organizations explicitly endorsing the teaching of evolution, the scientific community is behind them. With their professional organizations like the National Science Teachers Association and the National Association of Biology Teachers fully committed to supporting the teaching of evolution, the educational community is behind them, too.

And in a controversy dominated by a polarizing science-versus-religion stereotype, it is often insufficiently appreciated that a substantial portion of the faith community also supports the teaching of evolution. Entire denominations, such as the Episcopal Church, the United Methodist Church and the Presbyterian Church (USA), have issued statements affirming the compatibility of their faith and evolution, for example, while more than 16,000 individual clergy of the Christian, Jewish, Unitarian and Buddhist faiths have joined a grassroots effort to do the same.

Even time is arguably on the side of teaching evolution. Adapting Theodore Parker's majestic words, the philosopher Barbara Forrest recently wrote, "The arc of history bends toward teaching evolution."

American attitudes, she suggests, are changing in a way that offers hope for the increased acceptance of teaching evolution. And survey results support her argument: in 2017, Gallup reported that acceptance of creationism is at its lowest point measured in 35 years, with only 38 percent of Americans believing that God created humans in their present form within the last 10,000 years.

But success is not inevitable. It took the efforts of a host of dedicated science teachers—Susan Epperson in Little Rock, Arkansas, and before her, John Scopes in Dayton, Tennessee, and after her, Donald Aguillard in Lafayette, Louisiana, and hundreds and thousands of unsung heroes of science education in the background—to ensure that evolution is taught as well as it is today. It will take the efforts of their successors to ensure that it is taught even better in the future. And it will take the support of all of us who value the integrity of science education to enable them to do so.

The views expressed are those of the author(s) and are not necessarily those of Scientific American.

About the Author

Glenn Branch is deputy director of the National Center for Science Education, a nonprofit organization that supports the accurate teaching of evolution and climate change.

Evolution Education in the U.S. Is Getting Better

By Glenn Branch and Ann Reid

Woo-hoo, d'oh, or *meh*? Which of these Simpsonian reactions is appropriate to the fact, revealed by a 2019 survey conducted by researchers at Penn State University and the National Center for Science Education (NCSE), that about two in three 67 percent of public high school biology teachers are presenting evolution forthrightly, emphasizing the broad scientific consensus on evolution while not giving any credence to creationism? Only in the context of the long and contentious history of evolution education in the United States is it clear what the most plausible answer is.

American teachers have not always been afforded the luxury of teaching evolution forthrightly. John Thomas Scopes, for example, was famously prosecuted for violating Tennessee's ban on teaching evolution in 1925. Although his conviction was subsequently overturned, a national survey of high school biology teachers conducted in 1939–1940 revealed that only about half were teaching evolution as a central principle of biology. And bans on teaching evolution remained in place in Arkansas, Mississippi and Tennessee until 1970.

New obstacles then emerged, particularly requirements to teach various forms of creationism as alternatives to evolution. As recently as 15 years ago, in Dover, Pennsylvania, the local school board attempted to require its high school biology teachers to read a statement to their ninth-grade students describing "Darwin's theory of evolution" as "not a fact," and commending "intelligent design"—then a trendy slogan for creationism—to their attention as a scientifically credible alternative. The teachers, to their credit, unanimously refused to comply.

But their refusal, together with the controversy surrounding the related trial over the constitutionality of the board's actions, *Kitzmiller v. Dover*, intrigued two parents a hundred miles to the northwest, in State College, Pa. Michael Berkman and Eric Plutzer were not just any concerned parents, though: they were political scientists at Penn State with a particular interest in education policy. What—they wondered—are high school biology teachers teaching about evolution, and what factors influence their teaching practices?

To satisfy their curiosity, Berkman and Plutzer conducted the first modern national survey of high school biology teachers in 2007. The results were dire. Only a slight majority, 51 percent, reported that they emphasized the broad scientific consensus on evolution while not giving any credence to creationism, as if to suggest no progress in the 67 years since the less rigorous survey of 1939–1940. That's why the results of the 2019 survey—a collaboration between Plutzer and the NCSE—are so encouraging.

Between 2007 and 2019, there definitely was progress: from 51 percent of high school biology teachers reporting emphasizing evolution and not creationism in 2007 to 67 percent in 2019. It was matched by a drop from 23 to 12 percent of teachers who offer mixed messages by endorsing both evolution and creationism as a valid scientific alternative to evolution, from 18 to 15 percent of teachers who endorse neither evolution nor creationism, and from 8.6 to 5.6 percent of teachers who endorse creationism while not endorsing evolution.

What accounts for the improvement? Did intelligent design's crushing defeat in the *Kitzmiller* trial make the difference? Probably not. Science teachers are guided not by case law but by state science standards, which specify what students in the state's public schools are expected to learn. Standards thus influence the content of textbooks, statewide testing, and coursework for pre-service and in-service teachers. Importantly, they also provide a shield for teachers facing misguided community pressure over socially contentious topics like evolution.

The results of the 2019 survey suggest that a concerted effort to improve state science standards helped to improve evolution education. The Next Generation Science Standards (NGSS), which debuted in 2013, include "Biological Evolution: Unity and Diversity" as a disciplinary core idea of the life sciences at the middle and high school levels. By now, 20 states (plus the District of Columbia) have adopted the NGSS, and a further 24 states have adopted standards based on the same evolution-friendly framework on which the NGSS are based.

Were states that adopted the NGSS especially hospitable to the teaching of evolution? Not really: in 2007, their teachers were less likely to endorse evolution and not creationism than the national average. By 2019, they were more likely. While a variety of explanations are possible, teachers in NGSS states reported having taken more pre-service and in-service coursework in evolution than their colleagues elsewhere, suggesting that the increased expectations impelled both novice and veteran teachers to upgrade their content knowledge of evolution.

Despite the encouraging trend over a mere dozen years, there is still reason for concern: after all, more than one in six high school biology teachers, 17.6 percent, are still presenting creationism as a scientifically credible alternative to evolution. And almost as many high school biology teachers, 15 percent, are still failing to emphasize the broad scientific consensus on evolution, despite its general prevalence in state science standards and despite encouragement from professional organizations. *D'oh!*

With 13,500-odd local school districts having primary responsibility for curriculum and instruction, changes to science education are inevitably going to be slow, scattered and incremental. Still, with the aid of uncounted scientists, educators, policymakers, administrators and concerned citizens in general (and perhaps even a certain episode of *The Simpsons*), clear and convincing improvements for evolution education were demonstrably attained in just a dozen years. It is a victory worth not only celebrating–*woo-hoo!*–but also enlarging upon.

About the Authors

Glenn Branch is deputy director and Ann Reid is executive director of the National Center for Science Education, a nonprofit organization that supports the accurate teaching of evolution and climate change.

Science Education Is Under Legislative Attack

By Glenn Branch

Nearly a quarter of a million science teachers are hard at work in public schools in the United States, helping to ensure that today's students are equipped with the theoretical knowledge and the practical knowhow they will need to flourish in tomorrow's world. Ideally, they are doing so with the support of the lawmakers in their state's legislatures. But in 2019 a handful of legislators scattered across the country introduced more than a dozen bills that threaten the integrity of science education.

It was a mixed batch, to be sure. In Indiana, Montana and South Carolina, the bills sought to require the misrepresentation of supposedly controversial topics in the science classroom, while in North Dakota, Oklahoma and South Dakota, their counterparts were content simply to allow it. Meanwhile, bills in Connecticut, Florida and Iowa aimed beyond the classroom, targeting supposedly controversial topics in the state science standards and (in the case of Florida) instructional materials.

Despite their variance, the bills shared a common goal: undermining the teaching of evolution or climate change. Sometimes it is clear: the one in Indiana would have allowed local school districts to require the teaching of a supposed alternative to evolution, while the Montana bill would have required the state's public schools to present climate change denial. Sometimes it is cloaked in vague high-sounding language about objectivity and balance, requiring a careful analysis of the motives of the sponsors and supporters.

Either way, though, such bills would frustrate the purpose of public science education. Students deserve to learn about scientific topics in accordance with the understanding of the scientific community. With the level of acceptance of evolution among biomedical scientists at 99 percent, and the level of acceptance of climate change among climate scientists not far behind at 97 percent, it is a disservice to students to misrepresent these theoretically and practically important topics as scientifically controversial.

The National Science Teaching Association agrees. In its position statement on the teaching of evolution, the NSTA describes evolution as "a major unifying concept in science" that "should be emphasized in K–12 science education frameworks and curricula." Similarly, in its position statement on the teaching of climate science, the NSTA recommends that teachers of science "emphasize to students that no scientific controversy exists regarding the basic facts of climate change."

Why, then, do legislators who should be trying to support science teachers introduce bills reflecting their own half-baked notions about science? Presumably in the service of gratifying ideologies—usually religious in the case of evolution; usually political in the case of climate change—to which they, and their constituencies, subscribe. That also helps to answer the question of why they introduce such bills even when the bills are—as in Connecticut, Indiana, Iowa, Montana and South Carolina—unlikely to be enacted.

But complacency about bills such as those in the current baker's dozen is unwarranted. Sometimes, after all, they succeed in passing. Louisiana and Tennessee passed laws in the last decade similar to the bills introduced this year in North Dakota, Oklahoma, and South Dakota, for example, and Florida recently passed a law enabling ideologically motivated challenges to instructional materials, which two of the three bills introduced there this year sought to expand further.

Moreover, the introduction of even the most hopeless of bills in a state legislature sends a message to teachers: that teaching evolution and climate change is unwelcome. Common sense suggests, and survey research confirms, that public school teachers are leery of teaching topics that they believe are regarded as controversial in their communities. Merely by taking a public stand against evolution and climate change, legislators may discourage educators from teaching these topics properly.

If public school science educators are not able to teach evolution and climate change honestly, accurately and confidently, then the scientific literacy of millions of students in America's public schools is going to be in jeopardy. The lawmakers of the 50 state legislatures are responsible for supporting these teachers properly. It is up to us, their constituents, to ensure that they do—and to reproach them when they introduce their half-baked ideas to the contrary.

The views expressed are those of the author(s) and are not necessarily those of Scientific American.

About the Author

Glenn Branch is deputy director of the National Center for Science Education, a nonprofit organization that supports the accurate teaching of evolution and climate change.

Section 3: Evolution Before Our Eyes

3.1 That Mouse in Your House—It's Smarter, Thanks to You
By Christopher Intagliata

3.2 The Mangrove Finch: An Extinction in Slow Motion
By John R. Platt

3.3 Humans Make Wild Animals Less Wary
By Jason G. Goldman

3.4 Malaria Mosquitoes Are Biting before Bed-Net Time
By Jason G. Goldman

That Mouse in Your House—It's Smarter, Thanks to You

By Christopher Intagliata

Scientists studied three varieties of house mice and found that those who had lived alongside humans the longest were also the craftiest at solving food puzzles. Christopher Intagliata reports.

If you've ever hosted a mouse as a houseguest, you know they can be incredibly clever at finding your food. And that makes sense.

"They had to become better in traits like problem solving because we became better at hiding our food from them."

Anja Guenther is with the Max Planck Institute in Germany. She says that battle of the minds has made mice craftier over time.

"The longer the mice lived with humans, the better they are at problem-solving."

You see, there are more than a dozen subspecies of house mice worldwide. And each began cohabitating with humans at different times in our evolutionary history. For example ...

"Mus musculus domesticus."

It began raiding human pantries around 12,000 years ago.

"Mus musculus musculus"

Our relationship with them began some 8,000 years ago.

"And *Mus musculus castaneus."*

It's a relative newcomer who began cohabitating only 3,000 to 5,000 years ago.

And that spread in evolutionary life histories, with constituents from all three groups, gave Guenther's team an opportunity. They gathered 150 mice—representing all three groups—and tested them with seven different food puzzles. Each puzzle was baited with a mealworm, which the mice could only get by pushing or pulling a lid, for example, or extracting a ball of paper from a tube or opening the window of a Lego house.

And they found that the *longer* a mouse variety had lived with humans, the more likely it was to solve these food puzzles.

"So, basically, what we are left at, with trying to explain these results that we see, is that the mice really developed higher enhanced cognitive abilities while living with humans."

The results appear in the *Proceedings of the Royal Society B.*

As the human footprint on the globe expands, Guenther says it's more important than ever to understand how we influence animal minds to learn why some creatures, like housemice, adapt while others simply die out.

[The above text is a transcript of this podcast.]

About the Author

Christopher Intagliata is a science writer and audio journalist whose work appears on Science Friday, Scientific American, *NPR and more.*

The Mangrove Finch: An Extinction in Slow Motion

By John R. Platt

One of Charles Darwin's fabled finch species is slowly disappearing, even as conservationists work desperately to save it.

This "slow-motion extinction," as a newly published paper puts it, concerns the critically endangered mangrove finch (*Camarhynchus heliobates*). Native to the Galápagos Islands, the species has found itself plagued by invasive species for decades. The finches have completely vanished from one of their homes, Fernandina Island, and now survive in just one small population of 80 to 100 birds on the west coast of Isabel Island.

Conservationists working to preserve this species have done a good job recently managing the invasive rats and parasitic flies that took a toll on mangrove finch populations, but the new research reveals that the crisis has had a lasting after-effect. The birds on Isabel Island now have half of the genetic diversity that they had a century ago.

This news was actually kind of expected. "We weren't particularly surprised by the low level of current genetic diversity, knowing that the last remaining population has been at critically low population size for quite some time, and nearly decimated by the rats and flies," says the study's lead author, Lucinda Lawson with the University of Cincinnati.

In fact, that low diversity may actually be the legacy of historically low population sizes for the species. "It seems clear that mangrove finches were probably always a marginalized species living in the tiny and ephemeral mangrove forests ringing the edges of these two islands," Lawson says. "Altogether, there probably haven't been sufficient population sizes within the history of this species to maintain significant genetic diversity."

But the researchers also discovered something else in their genetic tests. It turns out the mangrove finches are breeding and hybridizing with another species, the woodpecker finch (*C. pallidus*). The two species share an overlapping range and look remarkably alike. Other than the males' different breast colors and different songs, they're almost impossible to tell apart.

Again, this hybridization was anticipated because previous researchers had captured a few individuals that seemed to have traits of each species. Still, Lawson says they were surprised by the number of hybrids that they found and that the genetics indicated they've been breeding for at least two generations.

Another surprise came when they investigated a nest of chicks being reared by a mangrove finch father. You'd think the nest would have mangrove finch chicks, right? Well, they turned out to be unrelated woodpecker finches.

How did this cross-species parenting come to be? "To purely speculate on the situation, it's possible that the female was a woodpecker finch who shared a nest with a male mangrove finch, yet was involved in extra-pair paternity with a woodpecker finch, so the pure woodpecker babies raised by a mangrove 'father,'" Lawson says. "It's only one small story within the larger dataset, but it's an interesting anecdote when evaluating mating within a 'dying' population."

Lawson says all of this hybridization probably isn't hurting the chicks, unlike some other species where hybridization can create sterile or unhealthy young (mules, for example). The two species are closely related, she points out, and they have very small differences between them, mostly focused on small variances in beak shape. Other Darwin's finch species have also hybridized with less success since the mixing of beak sizes left hatchlings less able to feed themselves.

The hybridized mangrove and woodpecker finches may have even given themselves an advantage over the parasitic fly, *Philornis downsi*, which sucks the blood out of birds during its larval form. Other research has shown that hybrid nests have fewer flies, so perhaps the hybrids gained a specialization that they could use to defend themselves.

Even though the few mangrove finches that remain continue to face threats, Lawson says she has hope. "Other bird species have bounced back from near extinction, and there's no reason to think that these couldn't as well if their immediate threats are kept in check," she says, noting in particular the efforts of the Charles Darwin Foundation to control *P. downsi* levels. "It seems to me that if they can get the flies under control—which they are making some progress on—and keep the rats away, then they may be able to maintain this species and possible see the population grow."

On the other hand, maybe this slow-motion extinction will result in the mangrove finch continuing to hybridize and being "absorbed" by its related species. "In such a way the mangrove finch would 'live on' within the woodpecker finches much as Neanderthals and Denisovans live on within *Homo sapiens*," Lawson says. "I don't think this potential merging of species should be seen as a particularly negative outcome if it does come about."

Beyond that, she says it's "not unlikely" that Galápagos finch species have been born and reabsorbed several times over the history of the landscape.

If the mangrove finch eventually disappears, it's probably something that will continue to happen in dribs and drabs, in slow motion, which conservationists from around the world watch closely as they vanish. Or maybe they'll save it through ongoing captive breeding or other efforts. Either way, it's likely something we'll be following this in slow motion for several years yet to come.

The views expressed are those of the author(s) and are not necessarily those of Scientific American.

About the Author

John R. Platt is the editor of The Revelator. *An award-winning environmental journalist, his work has appeared in* Scientific American, Audubon, Motherboard, *and numerous other magazines and publications. His "Extinction Countdown" column has run continuously since 2004 and has covered news and science related to more than 1,000 endangered species. John lives on the outskirts of Portland, Ore., where he finds himself surrounded by animals and cartoonists.*

Humans Make Wild Animals Less Wary

By Jason G. Goldman

From mammals to mollusks, animals living among humans lose their antipredator behaviors.

Wild animals are equipped with a variety of techniques to avoid becoming lunch for a bigger, toothier animal. The most well-known methods include the classic "fight" and "flight," as well as "freeze." A team of researchers wondered how proximity to people might impact those survival strategies.

"We often see that animals are more tolerant around us in urban areas, but we don't really know why."

U.C.L.A. evolutionary biologist Dan Blumstein.

"Is it a filtering process where only the tolerant animals are there? Is it individual plasticity, meaning individuals change their fear of us, and that leads to tolerance? Or can there be an evolutionary dynamic occurring?"

To find out, Blumstein and colleagues combined information from 173 studies of more than 100 species, including mammals, birds, reptiles, fish and even mollusks. Turns out that regardless of evolutionary lineage, the animals react in a similar way to life among humans: they lose their antipredator traits. That pattern is especially pronounced for herbivores and for social species.

This behavioral change is perhaps unsurprising when it's intentional, the result of domestication and a controlled breeding paradigm. But it turns out that urbanization alone results in a similar change, though much more slowly–around three times more slowly. The results are in the journal *PLOS Biology*.

"The main point is: we're essentially domesticating animals by urbanization. We're selecting for the same sorts of traits that we would if we were actually trying to domesticate them."

If the urbanization process helps animals better coexist with people, it could be to their benefit. But if it makes them more vulnerable to their nonhuman predators, it could be a real problem.

Either way, these results mean that city living exerts enough of an influence on wild animals that evolutionary processes kick in. Those reductions in antipredator traits become encoded in their genes.

"We're changing the population genetics and changing genetic variation. We are reducing, we are eliminating variation. And if variation is a good thing and is a target of conservation, then that's something to be concerned with."

What the researchers now wonder is whether the mere presence of tourists in less urbanized areas can instigate similar changes in wild animals. If so, serious questions exist for the notion of ethical, welfare-oriented ecotourism. If we wish to help animals retain their antipredator defenses, the researchers say, we might have to intentionally expose animals to predators—or at least to predator-related cues.

"It's just yet one other way that we're changing the world around us."

[The above text is a transcript of this podcast.]

About the Author

Jason G. Goldman is a science journalist based in Los Angeles. He has written about animal behavior, wildlife biology, conservation, and ecology for Scientific American, Los Angeles *magazine, the* Washington Post, *the* Guardian, *the BBC, Conservation magazine, and elsewhere. He contributes to* Scientific American's *"60-Second Science" podcast, and is co-editor of* Science Blogging: The Essential Guide *(Yale University Press). He enjoys sharing his wildlife knowledge on television and on the radio, and often speaks to the public about wildlife and science communication.*

Malaria Mosquitoes Are Biting before Bed-Net Time

By Jason G. Goldman

More than 200 million people get malaria each year. And about half a million die—mostly in Africa, many of them children. And those staggering numbers are an improvement. Malaria deaths have been cut in half since 2000. In many places, a remarkably simple tool has led the fight: bed nets treated with a mild insecticide that stop mosquitoes from biting people in their sleep.

Both people and mosquitoes are pawns in the malaria transmission cycle. If an infected person gets bitten by a mosquito, the parasite gets picked up along within the blood meal. That mosquito can then transfer the parasite to the next person it bites. Bed nets help stop mosquitoes from easy attacks on motionless sleepers. But now some mosquitoes seem to be giving up the night shift.

"Malaria mosquitos in Africa tend to shift their biting behavior."

Entomologist Eunho Suh from Penn State University's Center for Infectious Disease Dynamics.

"Normally they tend to bite people during the night, but because of extensive use of bed nets, these mosquitoes started biting in the early evening or in the morning."

Suh and his team wanted to know whether observed change in biting time had any impact on malaria transmission. Back in the lab, they presented Anopheles mosquitoes with the opportunity to feed on blood at 6 P.M., at midnight and at 6 A.M. When the laboratory was kept at an even 80 degrees Fahrenheit, evening and morning biters were no more or less likely to become infectious than the midnight biters.

But in the real world of the warm and humid tropics, nighttime is slightly cooler than daytime. And when the researchers introduced that temperature variation, the evening biters were a lot more likely to have potent malaria parasites. The results are in the journal *Nature Ecology & Evolution*.

"Not all mosquito bites are equal. So mosquitoes biting in the evening can have the highest transmission potential, compared to mosquitoes biting at midnight or the morning."

Suh thinks that the difference in the likelihood of mosquitoes becoming infectious has to do with the way that the malaria parasite matures. The parasites have a tougher time developing when mosquitoes are too warm. But if a mosquito picks up the parasites from blood at around dusk, those parasites have more hours of cooler nighttime temps to complete their development.

Next, Suh wants to conduct a similar study of wild mosquitoes and wild malaria parasites in Africa to see if the results from his lab mosquitoes hold up.

Either way, bed nets will remain an important tool. But understanding the enemy's behavior is always crucial information in any battle.

[The above text is a transcript of this podcast.]

About the Author

Jason G. Goldman is a science journalist based in Los Angeles. He has written about animal behavior, wildlife biology, conservation, and ecology for Scientific American, Los Angeles *magazine, the* Washington Post, *the* Guardian, *the BBC, Conservation magazine, and elsewhere. He contributes to* Scientific American's *"60-Second Science" podcast, and is co-editor of* Science Blogging: The Essential Guide *(Yale University Press). He enjoys sharing his wildlife knowledge on television and on the radio, and often speaks to the public about wildlife and science communication.*

Section 4: Origins of Complex Life

4.1 The Noninevitability of Life
By Caleb A. Scharf

4.2 The First Gene on Earth May Have Been a Hybrid
By Andy Extance

4.3 New Clues about the Origins of Biological Intelligence
By Rafael Yuste and Michael Levin

4.4 Evolution's Favorite Fish Diversify through "Noncoding" Genes
By Jason G. Goldman

4.5 Fossils Reveal When Animals Started Making Noise
By Michael B. Habib

The Noninevitability of Life

By Caleb A. Scharf

The current flurry of actions and concerns to do with the spread of the COVID-19 virus across the human population has got me thinking about some of the curious ways we conceptualize the nature of life. Ways that, in many respects, are directly counter to how life appears to actually function.

For instance, when a nasty little pathogen like COVID-19 emerges, we naturally start trying to limit its spread and to find ways to eliminate it–through vaccination and social control. All completely reasonable. We also, I think, imagine the situation as a "war," a threat, and a thing to be corralled and directed. The virus is a fault in the system, a deviation from the pathway that we envisage for ourselves. In other words, it highlights the fact that we tend to think of the underlying biological nature of our life as something with rules, rights, and governance (religion doesn't help dissuade some of us from this).

Except that's not how it works. Evolution's directionality is mostly an illusion. For instance, while it's certainly true that on average the net complexity of life on Earth has increased in fits and starts, that may be solely in service of deeper physical drivers; not because complex life is somehow "better" than less complex life.

To back up for a moment: the living things that we see at any moment in time are there because they can be. These are the species whose traits have, for now, allowed their propagation into the future. There is no plan behind this, it's like an enormously complex elaboration of throwing a bunch of coins into the air and declaring all the ones that land heads-up the winners. The coins didn't plot this outcome, it happened because the vagaries of air currents, angular momentum, and each coin's microscopic variations. For life the major addition to this scenario is that those variations, the traits, can muddle through in replications of the current generation, and some will increase the odds of landing heads up again.

Complexification of life seems to happen in part because organisms that can sense, embody, and act on more information about the world around them increase their odds of being there in the future. They can move to food, avoid predators, and so on. Information processing requires increasingly complicated physical structures and mechanisms. But relentless biological experimentation, governed by the likelihood of continued existence, also explores an invisible landscape of free energy. Discovering opportunities to dissipate that energy and be swept along in the flow of the 2nd law of thermodynamics: There are vastly more possible futures of disorder and inaction than there are of order and action, thus the world moves towards thermodynamic equilibrium and greater entropy.

That combination of thermodynamic imperative and informational flow is potent and has, across billions of years, unlocked more and more ways to release and process energy—in biochemical reactions, in photons from the Sun, in re-engineering Earth's environments over and over.

Because of all of this it's tempting to say that life is all but inevitable. It's part of how the universe unpacks itself.

I suspect that is true, however it's *only* true in a statistical, average sense. After all, it's not like life on Earth has always been successful. There have been enormous extinction events, and enormous slow-rolling revolutions that have pushed certain kinds of life into peripheral, boutique niches. The example of oxygen-breathing organisms versus those for whom oxygen is toxic is a pretty instructive case. Life is also a system constantly in competition with itself, from predator and prey to host and parasite, and pathogen to victim. Sometimes those competitions can flame out, other times they push species in new directions.

Which connects things back to humans and COVID-19. While in no way diminishing the very real and immediate human suffering that is associated with this virus, or our reasonable efforts to contain and eliminate the threat, it is a fascinating example of this greater drama playing out on Earth. This virus—like many—will shift the nature of our species, maybe not by large amounts, but it will contribute to the unseen and complex spreadsheet of biological chance and contingency that computes the ripples of likelihood that spread into the future of our survival.

I'm not suggesting that the effects of this virus, biologically and socially, will contribute to the downfall of our species in some unanticipated way centuries from now. But it could. Equally, any of the trillions upon trillions of daily biological events and experiments taking place on Earth might be setting the world up for the next mass extinction. Perhaps making life less robust when yet another asteroid pounds into us (which will happen, it's simply a question of when). Or laying the pathway for some new form of pathogenic organism that takes the planet back from all those cumbersome multi-cellular species, resetting life to its enormously successful state some three billion years ago.

The views expressed are those of the author(s) and are not necessarily those of Scientific American.

About the Author

Caleb A. Scharf is director of astrobiology at Columbia University. He is author and co-author of more than 100 scientific research articles in astronomy and astrophysics. His work has been featured in publications such as New Scientist, Scientific American, Science News, Cosmos Magazine, Physics Today *and* National Geographic. *For many years he wrote the Life, Unbounded blog for* Scientific American.

The First Gene on Earth May Have Been a Hybrid

By Andy Extance

DNA and RNA, the two major modern forms of genetic code underpinning all of earthly biology, could have coexisted in strict pairings on our planet before life arose here, scientists in England, Scotland and Poland say. Using a hydrogen cyanide–based chemical system intended to mimic conditions in Earth's early history, the researchers made four bases, the molecular "letters" of the genetic alphabet. Strung together, these bases form gene sequences that cells translate into proteins. But surprisingly, the team found that of the four bases their experiments consistently made, two were in a form found in DNA, whereas the other two were of a kind seen in RNA.

The study, published in *Nature* and conducted by John Sutherland of the Medical Research Council Laboratory of Molecular Biology in Cambridge, England, and his colleagues, further undermines the so-called RNA world hypothesis. This idea, long one of the most prominent in origins-of-life research, posits that RNA formed the basis of Earth's biosphere long before DNA and other molecules important to life emerged. Yet to date, scant evidence has been found of chemical pathways to make the RNA-exclusive system that rigid versions of the idea adopt or that could lead to DNA. "People have tended to think of RNA as the parent of DNA," Sutherland says. "This [paper] suggests that they are molecular siblings."

Other scientists who were not involved with the study question the plausibility of the conditions used in this hydrogen cyanide-based route, however. Frances Westall, director of the exobiology group at the French National Center for Scientific Research's Center for Molecular Biophysics in Orléans, notes that forming the bases requires very specific conditions. Mixtures would need to dry out and be exposed to ultraviolet light—two hurdles most easily surmounted on dry land, which was in short supply during our planet's ocean-covered early days more than four billion years ago. "These conditions certainly existed on the early Earth," Westall says. "They would not have been that common because there was not that much exposed landmass." Although she adds that the study is "clever" and "not completely impossible," she concludes that "there are other, better hypotheses as to locations for the emergence of life and prebiotic molecules."

Arguments about plausibility have plagued the chemistry-based quest to understand life's beginnings on Earth since the early 1950s, when American researchers Stanley Miller and Harold Urey performed a landmark experiment. The pair simulated the effects of lightning in the early Earth's atmosphere and ocean by triggering electrical discharges in flasks containing hydrogen, water, ammonia and methane. Although their experiment famously produced sizable organic molecules vital for biochemistry, for decades other researchers have debated the plausibility of its conditions. Nevertheless, Miller and Urey's work showed that it was relatively simple to make important substances, such as the amino acids that link up to form proteins that perform myriad functions within living cells. Of particular relevance to origins-of-life studies, proteins can act as catalysts, enhancing and speeding up other chemical reactions that would otherwise be too slow or inefficient to plausibly occur. But proteins are not the only possible catalysts behind the rise of life on Earth.

In work that would ultimately net the 1989 Nobel Prize in Chemistry, molecular biologist Sidney Altman and biochemist Thomas Cech found that RNA—long considered merely an intermediate carrier of genetic information that is subservient to DNA—can also behave as a catalyst. The RNA world hypothesis suggests that such molecules could self-replicate, enabling early evolution before the existence of DNA and proteins. The idea, however, "was an overzealous, overenthusiastic response to a brilliant discovery," Sutherland says.

That response might have come partly because, to a naive chemist, it looks easy to leap from RNA to DNA. To create the long chains we often see coiled up into the DNA's iconic double helix, the bases are first connected to a "backbone" of sugar molecules. These combinations make up nucleosides: deoxyribonucleotides in DNA and ribonucleosides in RNA—which, unlike its DNA cousin, forms a single helix. The nucleosides do not use table sugar, or sucrose, but rather ribose in RNA and deoxyribose in DNA (the different sugars give each material its first initial). The distinction between the two sugar types is tiny: just one oxygen and one hydrogen atom. Yet that difference is enough for DNA and RNA to have distinct biological roles. And biochemically removing the atoms is far harder than simply erasing the letters representing them in a notebook.

Another flaw in the RNA world idea has been the difficulty of making ribose in the conditions that probably existed on the early Earth—and to then connect it to a base. Sutherland and his colleagues therefore sought more likely ways to make ribose sugars and ribonucleosides. One of their most promising approaches relied on two gases thought to have been relatively abundant in the planet's early atmosphere: hydrogen sulfide and hydrogen cyanide. When dissolved in water, bathed in ultraviolet light and subjected to cycles of drying, these simple compounds have produced many more complex molecules. They include amino acids and glycerol, the backbones of fatty molecules that can form cells' outer wall.

Sutherland took this approach a step further last year. Working with Ramanarayanan Krishnamurthy's team at the Scripps Research Institute in La Jolla, Calif., he and his colleagues showed that the ribonucleosides cytidine and uridine could be transformed into deoxyribose and the nucleoside and deoxyadenosine. Now—primarily via the efforts of team members Jianfeng Xu and Václav Chmela, both then at the Laboratory of Molecular Biology—the researchers have made even more progress. They mixed some of the intermediate molecules from the team's previous studies with salts such as sodium nitrite and magnesium chloride that could have been prevalent on the primordial Earth, then subjected them to acidic conditions and heat, respectively. Through these steps, the scientists found two possible routes to add a fourth base, the less common nucleoside inosine, to their preexisting collection. The addition was enough to make a four-letter genetic alphabet in which each base in a strand would exclusively pair with one of the other three letters in a second strand That base-pairing complementarity is how modern RNA and DNA works. But in the experiment, two letters came from RNA, and two came from DNA.

The arrangement "suggests that the chemistry to make RNA and DNA isn't as different as people have thought," Sutherland says. "People have tended to think of RNA coming before DNA and somehow then being taken over. This, to me, is suggesting that it's possible that you could have had an RNA-DNA hybrid, which could then give rise to the two separate molecules." Sutherland's team has not yet assembled the individual nucleosides and ribonucleosides into longer chains, however. Doing so is important, because showing that hybrid strands can really form and bind to a partner strand is crucial for moving the idea beyond speculation.

This is a key issue for Nicholas Hud, an origins-of-life researcher at the Georgia Institute of Technology, who was not involved in the study. He calls it an "excellent compilation of organic chemistry research" on water-based nucleoside synthesis. But Hud is not convinced that the paper resolves whether these nucleosides actually arose before living creatures. His own research suggests amino acids could have linked up to carry information and act as a catalyst before RNA. Hud thinks evolution would then have gradually produced the current genetic system over long stretches of geologic time. "If a molecule looks very difficult, from a chemical perspective, to make, yet it functions exquisitely in biology, then it's probably the case that it has been evolved over time," he says. For the same reasons, he is also skeptical about the RNA world hypothesis.

Furthermore, Hud sees the new study's reliance on rigid incremental steps, each performed in strict order and under carefully controlled conditions, as a significant weakness. If the order of the steps changed or certain products were not isolated, Sutherland

and his colleagues would have made much less of the substances they are interested in, Hud says. That caveat reduces the chances of the scenario unfolding in the chaotic environs of the early Earth.

Sutherland admits that, absent a time machine to travel back to life's true origins on our planet, "plausibility is everything" in this rarefied field of research. Even so, he firmly backs his team's work on establishing chemical routes to life's building blocks. "There are many, many fingers pointing at hydrogen cyanide," Sutherland asserts. "Does it prove that it all happened from hydrogen cyanide? It doesn't prove it. But it's good enough for me."

New Clues about the Origins of Biological Intelligence

By Rafael Yuste and Michael Levin

In the middle of his landmark book *On the Origin of Species*, Darwin had a crisis of faith. In a bout of honesty, he wrote, "To suppose that the eye with all its inimitable contrivances for adjusting the focus to different distances, for admitting different amounts of light, and for the correction of spherical and chromatic aberration, could have been formed by natural selection, seems, I confess, absurd in the highest degree." While scientists are still working out the details of how the eye evolved, we are also still stuck on the question of how intelligence emerges in biology. How can a biological system ever generate coherent and goal-oriented behavior from the bottom up when there is no external designer?

In fact, intelligence–a purposeful response to available information, often anticipating the future–is not restricted to the minds of some privileged species. It is distributed throughout biology, at many different spatial and temporal scales. There are not just intelligent people, mammals, birds and cephalopods. Intelligent, purposeful problem-solving behavior can be found in parts of all living things: single cells and tissues, individual neurons and networks of neurons, viruses, ribosomes and RNA fragments, down to motor proteins and molecular networks. Arguably, understanding the origin of intelligence is *the* central problem in biology–one that is still wide open. In this piece, we argue that progress in developmental biology and neuroscience is now providing a promising path to show how the architecture of modular systems underlies evolutionary and organismal intelligence.

Biologists are trained to focus on the mechanisms of living systems and not on their purpose. As biologists, we are supposed to work out the "how" rather than the "why," pursuing causality rather than goals. The "why" is not only always present but is precisely what drives specific "how"s to be chosen, enabling organisms to survive by selecting and exploiting specific mechanisms out of an astronomically large space of possibilities. In the case of the human eye, for example, the optical properties of the lens only make sense if they help focus the light on the retina. If you don't ask why the lens is transparent, you will never understand its function, no matter how long you study how it becomes transparent.

In fact, the problem of understanding how intelligence emerges is becoming more acute with the "omics" revolution, which is generating systematic, quantitative data on genomes, transcriptomes, proteomes and connectomes. Biological systems are being dissected into their ultimate complexity, but no magic answer is appearing at the end of the tunnel. The race to big data is not providing a better explanation of living systems. If anything, it's making it harder.

Modern biology faces a fundamental knowledge gap when trying to explain meaningful, intelligent behavior. How can a system composed of cells and electrical signals generate a well-adapted body with behavior and mental states? If cells are not intelligent, how can intelligent behavior emerge from a distributed system composed of them? This fundamental mystery permeates biology. All biological phenomena are, in a sense, "group decisions" because organisms are made of individual parts–organs, tissues, cells, organelles, molecules. What properties of living systems enable components to work together toward higher-level goals?

A common solution is emerging in two different fields: developmental biology and neuroscience. The argument proceeds in three steps. The first rests on one of natural selection's first and best design ideas: *modularity*. Modules are self-contained functional units like apartments in a building. Modules implement local goals that are, to some degree, self-maintaining and self-controlled. Modules have a basal problem-solving intelligence, and their relative independence from the rest of the system enables them to achieve their goals despite changing conditions. In our building example, a family living in an apartment could carry on their normal life and pursue their goals, sending the children to school for example, regardless of what is happening in the other apartments. In the body, for example, organs such as the liver operate with a specific low-level function, such as controlling nutrients in the blood, in relative independence with respect to what is happening, say, in the brain.

The second step in the argument is that modules can be assembled in a *hierarchy*: lower-level modules combine to form increasingly sophisticated higher-levels modules, which then become new building blocks for even higher-level modules, and so on. In our apartment building, families could belong to a local association, like a local chapter of a political party, whose goals could be to ensure the future welfare of all the families in the area. And this party could belong to a parliament, whose goal could be to shape the policy of the entire country, and so on. In biology, different organs could belong to the same body of an organism, whose goal would be to preserve itself and reproduce, and different organisms could belong to a community, like a beehive, whose goal would be to maintain a stable environment for its members. Similarly, the local metabolic and signaling goals of the cells integrate toward a morphogenetic outcome of building and repairing complex organs. Thus, increasingly sophisticated intelligence emerges from hierarchies of modules.

This may seem to solve the problem, except that hierarchical modularity still does not explain how evolution, changing solely one element at a time at a lower level, can ever manipulate the upper levels. Given that the upper levels are built with lower levers, wouldn't you still need to modify a slew of things at the same time to change an upper-level module? A third step in our argument addresses this problem: each module has a few key elements that serve as control knobs or trigger points that activate the module. This is known as *pattern completion*, where the activation of a part of the system turns on the entire system. In our apartment building, the family would have one central figure, let's say one of the parents, who would represent the family in meetings and engage it when needed. These trigger points serve to represent the entire module and thus enable these modules to be activated, altered, inactivated or deployed in novel circumstances without having to manipulate or recreate all their parts. Moreover, pattern completion naturally emerges from systems of interconnected elements with interactions among the elements.

In recent years, researchers have found evidence for pattern completion in both neural circuits and developmental biology. For example, when Luis Carrillo-Reid and his colleagues at Columbia University studied how mice respond to visual stimuli, they found that activating as few as two neurons in the middle of a mouse brain—which contains more than 100 million neurons—could artificially trigger visual perceptions that led to particular behaviors. These fascinating pattern-completion neurons activated small modules of cells that encoded visual perceptions, which were interpreted by the mouse as real objects. Similarly, in work published in 2018, Michael Levin of Tufts University and Christopher Martyniuk of the University of Florida reviewed data showing how triggering a simple bioelectric pattern in nonneural tissues induced cells to build an eye or other complex organs in novel locations, such as on the gut of a tadpole.

The idea of hierarchical modularity to explain biological intelligence has been explored before by economist Herbert Simon, neuroscientist Valentino Braitenberg, computer scientist Marvin Minsky, evolutionary biologists Leo Buss, Richard Dawkins and David Haig, and philosopher Daniel C. Dennett, among many others. These recent experiments from developmental biology and neuroscience can now provide a common mechanism of how this could work via key nodes that generate pattern completion. While there is still much to learn about how pattern completion units work, they could provide a solution to the problem of how to repurpose a system of modules without having to change it all. The manipulation of local goal-pursuing modules, to make them cooperate at multiple scales of organization in the body, is a powerful engine. It enables evolution to exploit the collective intelligence of cell networks, using and recombining tricks discovered at the lower level while operating with robustness despite noise and uncertainty.

Like a ratchet, evolution can thus effectively climb the intelligence ladder, stretching all the way from simple molecules to cognition. Hierarchical modularity and pattern completion can help understand the decision-making of cells and neurons during morphogenesis and brain processes, generating well adaptive animals and behavior. Studying how collective intelligence emerges in biology not only can help us better understand the process and products of evolution and design but could also be pertinent for the design of artificial intelligence systems and, more generally for engineering and even the social sciences.

Referenced

Imprinting and Recalling Cortical Ensembles. Luis Carrillo-Reid et al. in *Science*, Vol. 353, pages 691–694; August 12, 2016.

The Bioelectric Code: An Ancient Computational Medium for Dynamic Control of Growth and Form. Michael Levin and Christopher J. Martyniuk in *BioSystems*, Vol. 164, pages 76–93; February 2018.

Controlling Visually Guided Behavior by Holographic Recalling of Cortical Ensembles. Luis Carrillo-Reid et al. in *Cell*, Vol. 178, No. 2, pages 447–457; July 11, 2019.

The Computational Boundary of a "Self": Developmental Bioelectricity Drives Multicellularity and Scale-Free Cognition. Michael Levin in Frontiers in *Psychology*, Vol. 10, Article No. 2688 December 2019.

About the Authors

Rafael Yuste is a professor of biological sciences at Columbia University and director of its Neurotechnology Center.

Michael Levin is a biology professor and director of the Allen Discovery Center at Tufts University.

Evolution's Favorite Fish Diversify through "Noncoding" Genes

By Jason G. Goldman

Darwin's finches are perhaps the best-known examples of adaptive radiation—the evolutionary phenomenon in which one ancestral species rapidly diversifies into several new ones, each with unique adaptations for surviving in its own environment. But these Galápagos birds have nothing on the cichlids of East Africa. In the same two or three million years it took for 14 finch species to evolve, more than 1,000 cichlid species diverged from common ancestors in Lake Malawi alone. New research is now revealing the genetic mechanisms behind such rapid and dramatic biodiversity.

Cichlids exhibit a wild variety of body shapes, coloration patterns, mouth structures, behaviors, diets, and more. "When you look at them, they look so starkly different," says Earlham Institute evolutionary biologist Tarang Mehta. "But when you compare the [protein-coding] genes of these species, you see very little diversity."

Protein-coding genes influence an organism's major traits. Previous research had already indicated that cichlids' "noncoding" or "regulatory" stretches of DNA—which determine how, when and where the coding genes are turned on and off—evolved more rapidly than their coding genes. These regulatory spans let the same set of genetic puzzle pieces fit together in thousands of different configurations, a phenomenon Mehta refers to as "tinkering." But scientists were unsure whether this tinkering could drive the evolution of new species.

For a study published in *Genome Biology*, Mehta and his colleagues analyzed gene expression in the brain, eye, heart, kidney, muscle tissue and testis of five cichlid species from East African rivers and lakes. Using a computational model they developed, the researchers found that changes in the genomes' noncoding regions contributed a "substantial portion of the evolutionary substrate in adaptations" that led to divergence, says study senior author and University of East Anglia biologist Federica Di Palma. For example, the team found that regulatory changes altered certain coding genes' expression to let cichlids see better in various specific conditions. When species shared similar diets or habitats, they were more likely to evolve similar changes to these regulatory networks.

Many biologists worry about the accelerating loss of Earth's biodiversity—but science still does not fully understand how biodiversity evolves in the first place, says University of Basel zoologist Walter Salzburger, who was not involved with the study. The cichlids in Lakes Malawi, Tanganyika and Victoria offer researchers a unique opportunity to peer into that process, he adds.

Mehta's team is now applying the same kind of analysis to tilapia, a cichlid group that includes the world's second-most farmed fish. If the researchers can identify the genomic tinkering associated with traits such as adaptation to extreme salinity or temperature, Mehta says, this could guide the selective breeding of tilapia to more efficiently feed a hungry world.

About the Author

Jason G. Goldman is a science journalist based in Los Angeles. He has written about animal behavior, wildlife biology, conservation, and ecology for Scientific American, Los Angeles *magazine, the* Washington Post, *the* Guardian, *the BBC, Conservation magazine, and elsewhere. He contributes to* Scientific American's *"60-Second Science" podcast, and is co-editor of* Science Blogging: The Essential Guide *(Yale University Press). He enjoys sharing his wildlife knowledge on television and on the radio, and often speaks to the public about wildlife and science communication.*

Fossils Reveal When Animals Started Making Noise

By Michael B. Habib

We take it for granted that virtually every habitat on Earth is alive with the sounds of animals, from the haunting songs of whales in the oceans to the riotous symphony of birds, frogs and insects in forests to the hubbub of humans and our technological creations in cities the world over. Yet for most of our planet's history the only sounds were those of the wind, rain and waves.

In my work as a paleontologist, I seek to understand the lives of extinct animals—how they moved, what they ate, the sounds they might have made. I also serve as an animation and creature-design consultant for exhibits, television, movies and games. Among the most common topics I have been asked to tackle for these projects are those pertaining to animal sounds. Whether someone is reconstructing long-vanished pterosaurs for an academic study or designing a creature for a blockbuster film, sound is paramount in bringing both past and imaginary worlds to life.

Recent insights into the evolution of animal acoustics have led to a new understanding of how our modern-day soundscapes came to be. Fossils reveal when the major types of sound-production—and sound-detection—structures appeared in the forerunners of today's invertebrate and vertebrate creatures. And in some cases, clever modeling has allowed scientists to re-create the ancient sounds themselves. Many details remain to be worked out, but we can now begin to piece together the dawn of the din.

Breaking the Silence

The fossil record indicates that life on Earth got its start 3.7 billion years ago. But those earliest organisms—including microbes and, much later, soft-bodied animals similar to today's jellies—were a quiet bunch. It was not until the evolutionary burst that occurred in the Cambrian period, between 541 million and 485.4 million years ago, that animals acquired some basic sound-making behaviors related to locomotion and predation. Yet even then the hush under water, where these creatures lived, was probably punctuated only by the skittering of arthropod feet across sand or the faint grinding of a cephalopod breaking a shell. Meanwhile the terrestrial realm remained essentially silent. More than 200 million years passed before the buzzing of insects started to fill the air, giving rise to an entirely new acoustic world.

The oldest-known putative insect dates to 408 million years ago and was probably soundless and deaf. Scientists do not know exactly when insects started to first make or hear sounds, but the fossil record provides a minimum date: a katydid from around 250 million years ago has the sound-producing anatomy characteristic of this group. The earliest-known fossils of cicada relatives also date to this time. These insects can generate exceptionally loud sounds by rapidly buckling and unbuckling drumlike structures on their bodies called tymbals. The sound-production structures are so well preserved in some insect fossils that researchers can reconstruct the songs the creatures sang in life. In 2011 a team led by Jun-Jie Gu, now at Sichuan Agricultural University in China, worked out that a specific ancient katydid emitted songs tuned to a frequency of 6.4 kilohertz, which is roughly an octave higher than Mariah Carey's highest recorded note.

For these earliest buzzing insects, the advantages of producing and hearing sound would have been numerous. They could communicate over distances, hear predators approach and perhaps even lure prey by mimicking the sounds of a target animal's potential mate. Sound offered a new means of attracting mates and in so doing gave rise to a new kind of biological battle: the evolution of the loudest.

Vertebrates probably began experimenting with sound in some limited form around the same time that insects started buzzing and chirping. Today's amphibians, reptiles and mammals all possess a larynx, or voice box, near the top of their airway. This fact suggests they inherited it from their last common ancestor, which would mean the larynx is nearly as old as land vertebrates themselves, going back 300 million years or so. It probably took millions of years for truly specialized or powerful vocalizations to evolve in these animals, however. Little is known about these early stages of vertebrate vocalization, not least because the larynx is made up of cartilage, which generally does not preserve well.

What we do know is that starting roughly 230 million years ago, during the Mesozoic era, vertebrate animals evolved a wide range of vocal abilities. That is when the world became truly loud. For example, frogs, with their rich repertoire of calls and songs, first showed up in the Mesozoic. Mammals also debuted around this time, and their characteristic chirps, growls and hisses probably evolved early on. Although we do not have much direct evidence of the sound-production apparatus in early mammals, we do have an exciting fossil record of their ears. The mammalian ear is unique, with three tiny bones in the middle ear, two of which are derived from bones that make up the jaw in most other vertebrates. These special ears are quite good at hearing high-frequency sounds, which could have helped the mammals find buzzing insect prey. These mammals might also have been capable of producing high-frequency sounds, allowing individuals to communicate with one another in a frequency range that few other animals could detect.

Among the most acoustically talented animals in the Mesozoic were the dinosaurs. In 1981 David Weishampel carried out one of the first reconstructions of a fossil animal's vocalization, working with the herbivorous, duck-billed dinosaur *Parasaurolophus*. This creature had a giant crest on its head that connected to its airway. Weishampel demonstrated that the crest made for an excellent resonating chamber. By taking into account the size and shape of the crest, he was able to estimate the sound repertoire of *Parasaurolophus* and reproduce it with a model he built. (To this day, Weishampel affectionately refers to that rig as his "honker.")

Increasingly sophisticated digital tools have made it possible to do this kind of in-depth analysis on many more specimens. Since 2008 Lawrence Witmer of Ohio University and his team have been using CT scans, along with fluid mechanics modeling, to assess sound production in various dinosaur species. They have discovered that the skulls of many dinosaurs contained complex chambers. Air flow through these spaces would have been correspondingly convoluted. The air flow helped to regulate body temperature, but it also might have enabled the animals to produce a wide array of sounds, including honks, bellows and trumpets.

Reconstruction of dinosaur vocalizations has long been a mainstay of the movie industry. The roars in films such as *Jurassic Park* are among the most famous portrayals of extinct-animal sounds. But Julia Clarke of the University of Texas at Austin and her colleagues found that the sounds of predatory dinosaurs such as *Tyrannosaurus rex* might have been more birdlike than mammal-like. Reporting on Clarke's work, some journalists wrote the fearsome tyrannosaurs might have "honked" rather than "roared." But before you begin picturing *T. rex* as a giant goose, it is worth noting the researchers meant "honk" from a biomechanics standpoint–a sound produced largely through the nose rather than the mouth, starting with the vibration of structures deep in the chest. Scaled to tyrannosaur size, that honk becomes a bass-baritone mega war trumpet. The beast could have sounded off with the full force of the entire brass section of the Los Angeles Philharmonic before entering battle armed with six-foot-long bone-crushing jaws.

Some dinosaurs were probably quite a bit less vocal than often portrayed, however. In the original *Jurassic Park*, the long-necked brachiosaurs trumpet like elephants. In reality, they were probably nearly voiceless. At most they might have been able to hiss. In all tetrapods–the group that includes the first land vertebrates and their descendants–the primary vocalizations in the larynx are controlled predominantly by the recurrent laryngeal nerve. This nerve always has the same strange configuration: it runs all the way down the neck, loops around large blood vessels in the upper and middle chest, and then runs back up the neck to the larynx. As a result, the signals for voice have to travel about twice the length of the neck.

For short-necked animals, including humans, the resulting delay in signal speed is trivial. But for a giant, long-necked dinosaur, this delay would be comparatively enormous—so much so, in fact, that there would be no way to properly control the rapid movement of the vocal cords during complex vocalizations such as honking or trumpeting. The next time you watch *Jurassic Park*, imagine honking hadrosaurs, trumpeting tyrannosaurs and hissing brachiosaurs.

In all likelihood, many dinosaurs were impressive vocalists. But one group in particular evolved some of the most sophisticated vocalizations of any animal. Members of this group still live among us: the birds. The earliest-known birds were identified from fossil deposits that are about 150 million years old, although their unique vocal abilities may have evolved somewhat later.

Birds have a special vocal structure called a syrinx. Their larynx is reduced, and the syrinx provides nearly all of their vocal control. Whereas the larynx resides at the top of the main airway, the syrinx sits at the bottom, where the trachea (aka the windpipe) branches out to the lungs. This anatomical arrangement offers several advantages. One of the most fundamental, described in 2019 by Tobias Riede of Midwestern University and his colleagues, is that it greatly improves the resonating efficiency. In other words, it produces more sound for the same energetic cost. Another advantage is that the syrinx can use the airstreams from the right and left lungs differently. Songbirds are particularly adept at this; the sounds from each side can be produced simultaneously or independently. In some cases, the two sides are specialized for different frequency ranges, enabling the bird to sing internal duets. The modern-day Hermit Thrush's beautiful song results from this capability.

Scientists do not yet have a firm grasp on the origins of the syrinx. The oldest avian syrinx discovered to date comes from a specimen of the extinct bird *Vegavis*, described in 2016 by Clarke and her colleagues. *Vegavis* lived during the latest part of the Cretaceous period, 66 million to 69 million years ago. But its syrinx was already fairly specialized, with its expanded resonating space and asymmetry associated with dual-sided sound production. A more primitive version of the organ could have originated earlier.

Interestingly, the other vertebrate fliers of the Mesozoic, the pterosaurs, did not have a syrinx. So contrary to what Hollywood might have us believe, pterosaurs did not sound like birds. They probably sounded more like other reptiles. They might have growled, hissed, clicked or even bill clacked, opening and closing their beaks to make a clattering sound. The bill clack from a giant pterosaur, one with a nine-foot-long skull, could have been deafening to a wide range of creatures at close range.

Seeing with Sound

With the arrival of the Cenozoic era, starting 66 million years ago, a whole new way of experiencing the world acoustically emerged: echolocation. Bats and whales appeared early in the Cenozoic, and both groups evolved this ability to see with sound. Echolocation requires quite a bit of sophisticated anatomy, though. To use echolocation, an animal has to produce a beam of sound, aim it in the desired direction, listen for the echoes, and then process those echoes to determine the distance, speed and general shape of whatever object the sounds bounce back from. It is a great trick for navigating and hunting in dark skies or murky waters.

Just like with light, the size of the smallest object that can be seen with echolocation is equal to half the wavelength of the emitted beam. Sound waves are much longer than light waves, however, so to get a decent picture of the environment or to see tiny insects, the emitter must produce very high-frequency sounds, which have shorter wavelengths than low-frequency sounds do. In bats, these calls, which are produced by the larynx and tongue, are typically far too high for us to hear. Human hearing maxes out at about 20,000 hertz, whereas bat calls range from about 10,000 to a staggering 200,000 hertz. We only ever hear the bats' lowest-frequency calls; they sound like high squeaks to us, but they are the equivalent of bass-baritone voices to them.

We know roughly when bats started echolocating because of characteristics of the ear anatomy in fossil bats. To hear the echoes of ultrasonic calls, bats need comparatively giant inner ears. The primary structure of hearing in the skull is called a cochlea. Both of your cochlea would fit on the face of a dime with room to spare. If your cochlea were the same relative size as a bat's, each would be about the size of a golf ball. The 50-million-year-old *Icaronycteris index* from western Wyoming is one of the earliest-known bats, and it already had skull characteristics associated with ultrasonic echolocation in living bats.

The evolution of echolocation in bats marked a major ecological revolution: vertebrates could now hunt insects on the wing in total darkness. After 275 million years, flying insects had nowhere to hide. Bats flourished as a result of this innovation. Today they make up roughly 25 percent of mammal species, and although some bats rely solely on vision to hunt, most of them echolocate.

As well as echolocation works in aerial environments, aquatic habitats are in some ways even more amenable to the use of reflected sound to determine where objects are in space. Water carries sound energy with far less signal loss per unit distance, giving aquatic echolocators a longer range than their aerial counterparts. High-frequency sounds always have reduced range compared with low-frequency sounds in the same environment, but in the water some dolphins can manage to make out objects with echolocation from as far as 650 feet away. The aerial bats, in contrast, cannot locate large objects more than 160 to 300 feet away; the range is much shorter for tiny insect prey.

Marine dolphins, such as the familiar bottlenose dolphin, can use echolocation to get a "first look" at long range in dark or cloudy water. River dolphins, such as those that live in the Amazon River, make even greater use of echolocation. The environment of these cetaceans is exceptionally murky. The river dolphins have smaller eyes and thus reduced visual acuity compared with other cetaceans, and they seem to rely heavily on echolocation to navigate and find food.

Marine mammals hold other sound records, too. If producing sound that travels as far as possible is the name of the game rather than trying to hear the echoes, then the best option is to use very low-frequency sounds. Big animals in aquatic environments have the natural advantage here. It is no surprise, then, that the champions of massive sonic range are the giant baleen whales. With larynxes up to two feet long and calls so low a human cannot hear them, some of these whales sing songs that can carry for hundreds, possibly thousands, of miles. Between the bats and the whales, the world is even noisier than we humans may realize.

The Language Revolution

Some 230 million years after the sounds of early mammals began to permeate the world, vocalization took on a new role with the evolution of human language. The anatomical prerequisites for language, including a larynx that can adjust rapidly and sophisticated integration of the larynx and tongue, seem to date back at least to the origin of our genus, *Homo*. This means human ancestors may have had some form of speech as early as 2.8 million years ago. Exactly when and in which *Homo* species language first originated remains a matter of debate, though. Language arose not only from the anatomy that enables speech but also from the capacity for symbolic thought. Most models suggest *Homo erectus*, which debuted around 1.8 million years ago, was the first human ancestor to use symbols. But fully formed human language, with its complex rules of grammar and syntax, might be unique to our own species, which would mean it originated within the past few hundred thousand years.

It is not just the possession of language that is so powerful: humans are unique in their abilities to teach, learn and record language. Although researchers have successfully taught some other primates to use sign language, none of these educated apes has ever taught this language to others of its species, even when given the opportunity. In one case, a chimpanzee at the Duke University primate facility who had been taught sign language was reunited with his troupe. He tried to use his new skill set to communicate with his fellow chimps. After a week of attempts, his keepers found him in a corner of the paddock, where he had isolated himself. When they asked him in sign language why he was not with the other chimps, he signed back, "Because they are insects."

Human language is one of the most impactful biological traits ever to have evolved. The formation of our social groups, societies and civilizations has been predicated on it. By coordinating our efforts through language, we have invented everything from agriculture to space shuttles–technologies that themselves contribute to contemporary soundscapes. Ours may not be the earliest animal sound, or the loudest, or the sweetest, but it is, in a sense, the one that most changed the world.

About the Author

Michael B. Habib is a paleontologist and biomechanist at the Natural History Museum of Los Angeles and the Greater Los Angeles Zoo Association. He studies the anatomy and motion of pterosaurs, birds and feathered dinosaurs.

Section 5: Human Evolution

5.1 How Scientists Discovered the Staggering Complexity of Human Evolution
By Kate Wong

5.2 How a 380-Million-Year-Old Fish Gave Us Fingers
By John A. Long and Richard Cloutier

5.3 Fossils Upend Conventional Wisdom about Evolution of Human Bipedalism
By Jeremy DeSilva

5.4 Rockshelter Discoveries Show Neandertals Were a Lot like Us
By David W. Frayer and Davorka Radovcic

5.5 Mind Your "Fs" and "Vs": Agriculture May Have Shaped Both Human Jaws and Language
By Anne Pycha

How Scientists Discovered the Staggering Complexity of Human Evolution

By Kate Wong

In 1859, 14 years after the founding of this magazine, Charles Darwin published the most important scientific book ever written. *On the Origin of Species* revolutionized society's understanding of the natural world. Challenging Victorian dogma, Darwin argued that species were not immutable, each one specially created by God. Rather life on Earth, in all its dazzling variety, had evolved through descent from a common ancestor with modification by means of natural selection. But for all of Darwin's brilliant insights into the origins of ants and armadillos, bats and barnacles, one species is conspicuously neglected in the great book: his own. Of *Homo sapiens*, Darwin made only a passing mention on the third-to-last page of the tome, noting coyly that "light will be thrown on the origin of man and his history." That's it. That is all he wrote about the dawning of the single most consequential species on the planet.

It was not because Darwin thought humans were somehow exempt from evolution. Twelve years later he published a book devoted to that very subject, *The Descent of Man*. In it, he explained that discussing humans in his earlier treatise would have served only to further prejudice readers against his radical idea. Yet even in this later work, he had little to say about human origins per se, instead focusing on making the case from comparative anatomy, embryology and behavior that, like all species, humans had evolved. The problem was that there was hardly any fossil record of humans at that time to provide evidence of earlier stages of human existence. Back then, "the only thing you knew was what you could reason," says paleoanthropologist Bernard Wood of the George Washington University.

To his credit, Darwin made astute observations about our kind and predictions about our ancient past based on the information that was available to him. He argued that all living humans belong to one species and that its "races" all descended from a single ancestral stock. And pointing to the anatomical similarities between humans and African apes, he concluded that chimpanzees and gorillas were the closest living relatives of humans. Given that relationship, he figured, early human ancestors probably lived in Africa.

Since then, Wood says, "the evidence has come in." In the past century and a half, science has confirmed Darwin's prediction and pieced together a detailed account of our origins. Paleoanthropologists have recovered fossil hominins (the group that comprises *H. sapiens* and its extinct relatives) spanning the past seven million years. This extraordinary record shows that hominins indeed got their start in Africa, where they evolved from quadrupedal apes into the upright-walking, nimble-fingered, large-brained creatures we are today.

And the archaeological record of hominin creations, which encompasses roughly half that time, charts their cultural evolution—from early experiments with simple stone tools to the invention of symbols, songs and stories—and maps our ancestors' spread across the globe. The fossils and artifacts demonstrate that for most of the period over which our lineage has been evolving, multiple hominin species walked the earth. Studies of modern and ancient DNA have generated startling insights into what happened when they encountered one another.

The human saga, we now understand, is far more intricate than scholars of yore envisioned. The tidy tropes of our prehistory have collapsed under the weight of evidence: there is no single missing link that bridges apes and humankind, no drumbeat march of progress toward a predestined goal. Our story is complicated, messy and random. Yet it still can be accommodated under Darwin's theory of evolution and in fact further validates that framework.

This is not to say scientists have it all figured out. Many questions remain. But whereas the origin of humans was once an uncomfortable speculation in Darwin's big idea, it is now among the best-documented examples of evolution's transformative power.

We humans are strange creatures. We walk upright on two legs and possess supersized brains, we invent tools to meet our every need and express ourselves using symbols, and we have conquered every corner of the planet. For centuries scientists have sought to explain how we came to be, our place in the natural world.

This quest was often distorted by racist ideologies. Consider the era leading up to the birth of Darwin's bombshell theory. In the 1830s, while a young Darwin was making his momentous voyage onboard the *Beagle*, a movement was underway to promote the idea that the various modern human groups around the globe—races—had separate origins. To build the case for polygenism, as the theory is known, scientists such as Samuel Morton in Philadelphia collected skulls from people across the world and measured their sizes and shapes, falsely believing those attributes to be proxies for intelligence. When they ranked the specimens from superior to inferior, Europeans would conveniently come out on top and Africans on the bottom. "There was a desire to provide scientific justification for political and power structures," says anthropological geneticist Jennifer Raff of the University of Kansas. "It was science in the service of slavery and colonialism."

Although Darwin's work came down firmly on the side of monogenism—the idea that all humans share a common ancestor—it was nonetheless co-opted to support notions about racial superiority. Social Darwinism, for one, misapplied Darwin's ideas about the struggle for existence in natural selection to human society, providing a pseudoscientific rationalization for social injustice and oppression. Darwin himself did not subscribe to such views. In fact, his opposition to slavery may have been a driving force in his research agenda, according to his biographers Adrian Desmond and James Moore.

By the time Darwin published *The Descent of Man*, in 1871, the idea that humans had evolved from a common ancestor with apes was already gaining traction in the scientific community thanks to books published in the 1860s by English biologist Thomas Henry Huxley and Scottish geologist Charles Lyell. Still, the fossil evidence to support this claim was scant. The only hominin fossils known to science were a handful of remains a few tens of thousands of years old that had been recovered from sites in Europe. Some were *H. sapiens*; others would eventually be recognized as a separate but very closely related species, *Homo neanderthalensis*. The implication was that fossils of more apelike human ancestors were out there somewhere in the world, awaiting discovery. But the suggestion by Darwin, like Huxley before him, that those ancestors would be found in Africa met with resistance from scholars who saw Asia as a more civilized birthplace for humankind and emphasized similarities between humans and Asia's gibbons.

Perhaps it should come as no surprise, then, that when the first hominin fossil significantly older and more primitive than those from Europe turned up, it came not from Africa but from Asia. In 1891 Dutch anatomist Eugène Dubois discovered remains on the Indonesian island of Java that he thought belonged to the long-sought missing link between apes and humans. The find, which he named *Pithecanthropus erectus*, spurred further efforts to root humankind in Asia. (We now know that Dubois's fossil was between 700,000 and one million years old and belonged to a hominin that was much more humanlike than apelike, *Homo erectus*.)

Two decades later the search turned to Europe. In 1912 amateur archaeologist Charles Dawson reported that he had found a skull with a humanlike cranium and an apelike jaw in an ancient gravel pit near the site of Piltdown in East Sussex, England. Piltdown Man, as the specimen was nicknamed, was a leading contender for the missing link until it was exposed in 1953 as a fraudulent pairing of a modern human skull with an orangutan's lower jaw.

Piltdown so seduced scholars with the prospect of making Europe the seat of human origins that they all but ignored an actual ancient hominin that turned up in Africa, one even older and more apelike than the one Dubois discovered. In 1925, 43 years after Darwin's death, anatomist Raymond Dart published a paper describing a fossil from Taung, South Africa, with an apelike braincase and humanlike teeth. Dart named that fossil–a youngster's skull now known to be around 2.8 million years old–*Australopithecus africanus*, "the southern ape from Africa." But it would take nearly 20 years for the scientific establishment to accept Dart's argument that the so-called Taung Child was of immense significance: the fossil linked humans to African apes.

Evidence of humanity's African origins has accumulated ever since. Every hominin trace older than 2.1 million years–and there are now quite a few of them–has come from that continent.

Even as fossil discoveries proved Darwin right about the birthplace of humanity, the pattern of our emergence remained elusive. Darwin himself depicted evolution as a branching process in which ancestral species divide into two or more descendant species. But a long-standing tradition of organizing nature hierarchically–one that dates back to Plato and Aristotle's Great Chain of Being–held sway, giving rise to the notion that our evolution unfolded in linear fashion from simple to complex, primitive to modern. Popular imagery reflected and reinforced this idea, from a caricature in *Punch's Almanack* for 1882 showing a progression from earthworm to Darwin, to the iconic monkey-to-man illustration that appeared in the 1965 Time-Life book *Early Man* and became known as the March of Progress.

From the rich assortment of fossils and artifacts recovered from around the world in the past century, however, paleoanthropologists can now reconstruct something of the timing and pattern of human evolution. The finds clearly show that this single-file scheme is no longer tenable. Evolution does not march steadily toward predetermined goals. And many hominin specimens belong not in our direct line of ancestry but on side branches of humankind–evolutionary experiments that ended in extinction.

From the outset, our defining traits evolved not in lockstep but piecemeal. Take our mode of locomotion, for example. *H. sapiens* is what anthropologists call an obligate biped–our bodies are built for walking on two legs on the ground. We can climb trees if we need to, but we have lost the physical adaptations that other primates have to arboreal life. Fragmentary fossils of the oldest known hominins—*Sahelanthropus tchadensis* from Chad, *Orrorin tugenensis* from Kenya and *Ardipithecus kadabba* from Ethiopia—show that our earliest ancestors emerged by around seven million to 5.5 million years ago. Although they are apelike in many respects, all of them exhibit characteristics associated with walking on two legs instead of four. In *Sahelanthropus*, for example, the hole in the base of the skull through which the spinal cord passes has a forward position suggestive of an upright posture. A bipedal gait may thus have been one of the very first traits that distinguished hominins from ancestral apes.

Yet our forebears appear to have retained traits needed for arboreal locomotion for millions of years after they first evolved the ability to walk on two legs. *Australopithecus afarensis*, which lived in eastern Africa from 3.85 million to 2.95 million years ago and is famously represented by the skeleton known as Lucy, discovered in 1974, was a capable biped. But it had long, strong arms and curved fingers—features associated with tree climbing. It would be another million years before modern limb proportions evolved and committed hominins to life on the ground, starting with early *H. erectus* in Africa (sometimes called *Homo ergaster*).

The brain evolved on quite a different schedule. Over the course of human evolution, brain size has more than tripled. A comparison of the braincase of *A. afarensis* with that of the much older *Sahelanthropus*, however, shows that hardly any of that growth occurred in the first few million years of human evolution. In fact, most of the expansion took place in the past two million years, perhaps enabled by a feedback loop in which advances in technology—stone tools and the like—gave hominins access to more nutritious foods such as meat, which could fuel a larger and thus more energetically demanding brain, which in turn could dream up even better technology, and so on. Shifts in the shape and structure of the brain accompanied these gains, with more real estate allocated to regions involved in language and long-range planning, among other advanced cognitive functions.

This mosaic pattern of hominin evolution in which different body parts evolved at different rates produced some surprising creatures. For instance, *Australopithecus sediba* from South Africa, dated to 1.98 million years ago, had a humanlike hand attached to an apelike arm, a big birth canal but a small brain, and an advanced ankle bone connected to a primitive heel bone.

Sometimes evolution even doubled back on itself. When one examines a hominin fossil, it can be difficult to discern whether the species retained a primitive trait such as small brain size from an earlier ancestor or whether it lost the characteristic and then re-evolved it. But the strange case of *Homo floresiensis* may well be an example of the latter. This member of the human family lived on the island of Flores in Indonesia as recently as 50,000 years ago yet looked in many ways like some of the founding members of our genus who lived more than two million years earlier. Not only did *H. floresiensis* have a small body, but it also possessed a remarkably tiny brain for Homo, about the size of a chimp's. Scientists' best guess is that this species descended from a brawnier, brainer *Homo* species that got marooned on Flores and evolved its diminutive size as an adaptation to the limited food resources available on its island home. In so doing, *H. floresiensis* seems to have reversed what researchers once considered a defining trend of *Homo*'s evolution: the inexorable expansion of the brain. Yet despite its small brain, *H. floresiensis* still managed to make stone tools, hunt animals for food and cook over fires.

Adding to the complexity of our story, it is now clear that for most of the time over which humans have been evolving, multiple hominin species walked the earth. Between 3.6 million and 3.3 million years ago, for example, at least four varieties of hominins lived in Africa. Paleoanthropologist Yohannes Haile-Selassie of Arizona State University's Institute of Human Origins and his colleagues have recovered remains of two of them, *A. afarensis* and *Australopithecus deyiremeda*, as well as a possible third creature known only from a distinctive fossil foot, in an area called Woranso-Mille in Ethiopia's Afar region. How they managed to share the landscape is a subject of current investigation. "Competing species could co-exist if there were plenty of resources or if they were exploiting different parts of the ecosystem," Haile-Selassie says.

Later, between roughly 2.7 million and 1.2 million years ago, representatives of our genus, *Homo*—large-brained tool users with dainty jaws and teeth—shared the grasslands of southern and eastern Africa with a radically different branch of humanity. Members of the genus *Paranthropus*, these hominins had massive teeth and jaws, flaring cheek bones and crests atop their heads that anchored powerful chewing muscles. Here the co-existence is somewhat better understood: whereas *Homo* seems to have evolved to exploit a wide variety of plants and animals for food, *Paranthropus* specialized in processing tough, fibrous plant foods.

H. sapiens overlapped with other kinds of humans, too. When our species was evolving in Africa 300,000 years ago, several other kinds of hominins also roamed the planet. Some, such as the stocky Neandertals in Eurasia, were very close relatives. Others, including *Homo naledi* in South Africa and *H. erectus* in Indonesia, belonged to lineages that diverged from ours in the deep past. Even as recently as 50,000 years ago, hominin diversity was the rule, with the Neandertals, the mysterious Denisovans from Asia, tiny *H. floresiensis* and another small hominin—the recently discovered *Homo luzonensis* from the Philippines—all at large.

Such discoveries make for a much more interesting picture of human evolution than the linear account that has dominated our view of life. But they raise a nagging question: How did *H. sapiens* end up being the sole surviving twig on what was once a luxuriant evolutionary bush?

Here are the facts of the case. We know from fossils found at the site of Jebel Irhoud in Morocco that our species originated in Africa by at least 315,000 years ago. By around 200,000 years ago it began making forays out of Africa, and by 40,000 years ago it had established itself throughout Eurasia. Some of the places *H. sapiens* colonized were occupied by other hominin species. Eventually the other folks all disappeared. By around 30,000 to 15,000 years ago, with the end of the Neandertals in Europe and the Denisovans in Asia, *H. sapiens* was alone in the world.

Researchers have often attributed the success of our species to superior cognition. Although the Neandertals actually had slightly larger brains than ours, the archaeological record seemed to indicate that only *H. sapiens* crafted specialized tools and used symbols, suggesting a capacity for language. Perhaps, the thinking went, *H. sapiens* won out by virtue of sharper foresight, better technology, more flexible foraging strategies and bigger social networks for support against hard times. Alternatively, some investigators have proposed, maybe *H. sapiens* waged war on its rivals, exterminating them directly.

But recent discoveries have challenged these scenarios. Neandertal technology, archaeologists have learned, was far more varied and sophisticated than previously thought. Neandertals, too, made jewelry and art, crafting pendants from shells and animal teeth and painting abstract symbols on cave walls. Moreover, they may not have been our only enlightened kin: a 500,000-year-old engraved shell from Java suggests that *H. erectus* also possessed symbolic thought. If archaic hominins had many of the same mental faculties as *H. sapiens*, why did the latter prevail?

The conditions under which *H. sapiens* got its start may have played a role. Fossil and archaeological data suggest that our species mostly stayed in Africa for the first couple of hundred thousand years of its existence. There, some experts argue, it evolved as a population of interconnected subgroups spread across the continent that split up and reunited again and again over millennia, allowing for periods of evolution in isolation followed by opportunities for interbreeding and cultural exchange. This evolutionary upbringing may have honed *H. sapiens* into an especially adaptable hominin. But that is not the whole story, as we now know from genetics.

Analyses of DNA have revolutionized the study of human evolution. Comparing the human genome with the genomes of the living great apes has shown conclusively that we are most closely related to chimpanzees and bonobos, sharing nearly 99 percent of their DNA. And large-scale studies of DNA from modern-day human populations across the globe have illuminated the origins of modern human variation, overturning the centuries-old notion that races are biologically discrete groups with separate origins. "There have never been pure populations or races," Raff says. Modern human variation is continuous, and most variation actually exists within populations rather than between them—the product of our demographic history as a species that originated in Africa with populations that mixed continuously as they migrated around the world.

More recently, studies of ancient DNA have cast new light on the world of early *H. sapiens* as it was when other hominin species were still running around. In the late 1990s geneticists began recovering small amounts of DNA from Neandertal and early *H. sapiens* fossils. Eventually they succeeded in getting entire genomes not only from Neandertals and early *H. sapiens* but also from Denisovans, who are known from just a few fragmentary fossils from Siberia and Tibet. By comparing these ancient genomes with modern ones, researchers have found evidence that our own species interbred with these other species. People today carry DNA from Neandertals and Denisovans as a result of these long-ago encounters. Other studies have found evidence of interbreeding between *H. sapiens* and unknown extinct hominins from Africa and Asia for whom we have no fossils but whose distinctive DNA persists.

Mating with other human species may have aided *H. sapiens*' success. Studies of organisms ranging from finches to oak trees have shown that hybridization with local species can help colonizing species flourish in novel environments by giving them useful genes. Although scientists have yet to figure out the functions of most of the genes people today carry from extinct hominins, they have pinpointed a few, and the results are intriguing. For instance, Neandertals gave *H. sapiens* immunity genes that may have helped our species fend off novel pathogens it encountered in Eurasia, and Denisovans contributed a gene that helped people adapt to high altitudes. *H. sapiens* may be the last hominin standing, but it got a leg up from its extinct cousins.

Scientists have many more pieces of the human-origins puzzle than they once did, but the puzzle is now vastly bigger than it was previously understood to be. Many gaps remain, and some may never close. Take the question of why we evolved such massive brains. At around 1,400 grams, the modern human brain is considerably larger than expected for a primate of our body size. "The singularity is why it's interesting—and why it's impossible to answer scientifically," Wood observes. Some experts have suggested that hominin brains ballooned as they adapted to climate fluctuations between wet and dry conditions, among other explanations. But the problem with trying to answer "why" questions about the evolution of our unique traits, Wood says, is that there is no way to evaluate the proposed explanations empirically. "There isn't a counterfactual. We can't go back to three million years ago and not change the climate."

Other mysteries may yield to further investigation, however. For example, we do not yet know what the last common ancestor of humans and the *Pan* genus that includes chimps and bonobos looked like. Genomic and fossil data suggest that the two lineages diverged between eight million and 10 million years ago—up to three million years before the oldest known hominin walked the earth—which means that paleoanthropologists may be missing a substantial chunk of our prehistory. And they have hardly any fossils at all of *Pan*, which has been evolving along its own path just as long as we have. Insights may come from a project currently underway in central Mozambique, where Susana Carvalho and René Bobe of the University of Oxford and their colleagues are hunting for fossil primates, including hominins, in sediments older than the ones that yielded *Sahelanthropus, Orrorin* and *Ardipithecus*.

Later stages of the human story are riddled with unknowns, too. If *H. sapiens* was interbreeding with the other hominin species it encountered, as we now know it was, were these groups also exchanging culture? Might *H. sapiens* have introduced Neandertals to novel hunting technology and artistic traditions—or vice versa? New techniques for retrieving ancient DNA and proteins from otherwise unidentifiable fossils and even cave sediments are helping researchers determine which hominin species were active and when at key archaeological sites.

One wonders where the next discovery will take us in the quest to understand who we are and where we come from. We may have found our place in nature, located our twig on the shrub, but we are still searching for ourselves. We're only human, after all.

About the Author

Kate Wong is a senior editor for evolution and ecology at Scientific American.

How a 380-Million-Year-Old Fish Gave Us Fingers

By John A. Long and Richard Cloutier

Five digits radiating from a palm, an arrangement both flexible and strong—capable of playing a piano, wielding a hammer, offering a comforting touch. The hand is our most familiar body part, central to most everyday tasks, from dressing and driving to cooking and texting. Yet from an evolutionary standpoint, it remains largely mysterious, particularly when it comes to the earliest stage of its origin. Other four-limbed creatures—tetrapods, as they are known—have hands that look and function quite differently than ours do. In birds and bats, they help to form delicate wings; in elephants, they support limbs as big around as tree trunks. But the basic structure is the same. In 1859 Charles Darwin remarked on the similarities in *On the Origin of Species*: "What can be more curious than that the hand of a man, formed for grasping, that of a mole for digging, the leg of the horse, the paddle of the porpoise, and the wing of the bat, should all be constructed on the same pattern, and should include the same bones, in the same relative positions?"

Darwin proposed an elegant explanation: these diverse animals share this pattern because they evolved from a common ancestor that possessed limbs with digits. In the more than 160 years since Darwin advanced his revolutionary idea, evolutionary biologists have marshaled evidence from paleontology, genetics and embryology that has proved him right. Their efforts have illuminated the shared ancestry of tetrapods, which evolved from fish; shown that the bones that make up the human hand are also found in frogs and birds and whales; and identified some of the genes that control the development of hands and wings and flippers, among other variations. But the first chapter of that story—the bit where the hand and wrist evolved from bones in the fin of an ancestral fish—has remained murky at best because scientists have lacked sufficiently complete fossils of transitional creatures between fully aquatic fish and land-roving tetrapods.

This past March we unveiled an extraordinary fossil—a complete skeleton of a 375-million-year-old fish, *Elpistostege watsoni*—that goes a long way toward filling that gap in understanding. The fossil preserves in its fins bones comparable to the ones that make up our fingers, showing that digits evolved before vertebrates left the water. This discovery overturns the conventional wisdom about when and how the hand evolved and shines new light on the rise of tetrapods, a pivotal event in the history of life on earth.

Murky Origins

Until recently, scientists' grasp of the evolutionary transition between fishes and early tetrapods hinged mainly on several spectacular fossils that seem to bridge these two groups. One is from a fish called *Panderichthys rhombolepis* from the Baltic region and dates to the Middle to Late Devonian period (around 384 million to 379 million years ago). With its elongated humerus and large radius and ulna (the upper arm bone and forearm bones, respectively, in tetrapods) and its tetrapodlike skull bone pattern, *Panderichthys* offered the first clues that the group of fishes to which it belongs were the closest fishes to the tetrapods. The group is called the elpistostegalians, after the then poorly known *Elpistostege* from eastern Canada.

In 2006 Neil Shubin of the University of Chicago and his colleagues announced the discovery of another elpistostegalian fish fossil, 380-million-year-old *Tiktaalik roseae* from the Canadian Arctic. *Tiktaalik* was a real game changer in revealing a slew of new data showing that the pectoral fin was highly advanced in these fishes—more so than any other known fossil—with both well-developed arm bones and mobile wrist joints. Its skull also had distinctive features, including a long, flat snout and a specialized braincase—traits shared by tetrapods.

Together, this and the other known elpistostegalian fish fossils suggested that a number of hallmark traits of tetrapods originated in their piscine predecessors, including land-worthy arm bones and joints. But what these fishes did not appear to have were fingers. In the case of *Panderichthys*, bony elements that many researchers initially thought were rudimentary digit bones were later rejected as such. And the *Tiktaalik* fossil, for its part, did not preserve the complete tip of the pectoral fin, where one would expect to find digit bones if the animal had them. The available evidence left experts to conclude that fingers were not part of the initial fin-to-limb transition. Instead they appeared to have evolved later, after tetrapods had already staked a claim on terra firma.

In science, however, knowledge is not written in stone. It is subject to change in light of fresh evidence. New discoveries can necessitate revision of the textbooks. Our recently described *Elpistostege* fossil, which was unearthed in 2010 at the UNESCO World Heritage Site of Miguasha in Quebec, is one such find. It is not a new species of elpistostegalian. Rather it is the original founding member of the band. But this time we have a complete, perfect specimen. And it has led us to propose a different theory of how fingers evolved and gave rise to the vertebrate hand structure that persists in the more than 33,800 species of tetrapods alive today, including humans.

To appreciate the role of *Elpistostege* in shifting our perspective on how hands evolved, it helps to know a bit about the history of its discovery. In the summer of 1937 two young British paleontologists were scouring the cliffs of Chaleur Bay along the southern shore of the windswept Gaspé Peninsula in eastern Canada. Thomas Stanley Westoll and William Graham-Smith were looking for Devonian-age fossils, and the cliffs were known to be an El Dorado for such treasures. Local collectors assisted the paleontologists in making their discoveries and sometimes sold them fossils. One of the fossils that Westoll purchased from them was a small, fragmentary skull roof that was to become a cornerstone in our understanding of the evolutionary transition between fishes and tetrapods.

Back in Westoll and Graham-Smith's day, scholars already suspected that tetrapods had evolved from the so-called lobe-finned fishes–creatures with fleshy, powerful fins, a group whose living representatives include the coelacanth and the lungfish. But they lacked fossils with intermediate anatomy to bolster the connection. Westoll's skull roof seemed like something that might help fill the gap. Given the pattern of its skull bones, Westoll thought it could be the long-sought-after skull of a primitive Devonian amphibian. He named this unique specimen *Elpistostege watsoni*, from the Greek for "hoped for" and "roof." In a brief paper published in 1938 in *Nature*, Westoll argued that the fossil provided "a perfect transition" between lobe-finned fishes and early four-legged animals.

Based on only a piece of skull, Westoll's argument was met with skepticism. More of the animal was needed. But although paleontologists came from all over Europe and America to collect fossils from the cliffs of Chaleur Bay, an area now designated Miguasha National Park, no one collected a new specimen of *Elpistostege*.

Some 30 years after Westoll's publication, however, serendipity intervened. Canadian fossil collector Allan Parent discovered the snout of an incomplete skull in the Miguasha Cliffs. It remained hidden in his private collection until his tragic early death. But in 1983 Parent's brother brought the snout to the attention of the Miguasha park director, Marius Arsenault, who in turn enlisted Hans-Peter Schultze, an eminent specialist on fossil fishes from the University of Kansas, to identify this unusual specimen. Schultze immediately realized its importance: similarities in the arrangement and shape of the cranial bones preserved in this fossil and Westoll's skull roof showed they belonged to the same species.

With more of the creature's anatomy revealed, ideas about its identity began to shift. The features visible on the new snout suggested that *Elpistostege* was not an amphibian but a highly advanced lobe-finned fish. In their 1985 paper describing the snout, Schultze and Arsenault specifically suggested that it was closely related to the Baltic fossil fish *Panderichthys*. They also discussed another enigmatic specimen, a fossil containing a patch of scales and some vertebrae that Miguasha chief biologist Marc Brassard and one of us (Cloutier) had found a couple of years earlier in the same cliffs. Considering the similarities in the surface textures of the scales preserved in this fossil and the snout, Schultze and Arsenault proposed that it, too, belonged to *Elpistostege*.

The attribution of the fossil containing the scales and vertebrae to *Elpistostege* was important. In addition to being the only material then known from below the creature's head, it had something the other two *Elpistostege* fossils did not: detailed provenance. The skull roof and snout were known to have been collected from the cliffs, but no one knew which rock layer they came from. In contrast, Brassard and Cloutier had recorded the exact stratigraphic location of the fossil they found: 90 meters above the lowermost layers of a distinctive geologic unit known as the Escuminac Formation.

In the years that followed, Cloutier and his collaborators returned to this part of the Escuminac Formation again and again to search for more remains of *Elpistostege*—to no avail. Still, the geologic and fossil evidence they did find allowed them to begin to reconstruct the animal's environment, a channel that fed into an estuary. A picture began to emerge of *Elpistostege* as the largest fish—and probably therefore the top predator—in the waters it shared with some 20 other species of fishes.

Eventually that paleoecological data would gain new relevance. Late in the afternoon of August 4, 2010, while on patrol in Miguasha, park warden and naturalist Benoît Cantin found an unusual piece of fossilized fish tail embedded in the lower Escuminac rock layers on the beach at the foot of the cliffs, less than 250 meters from the park's museum. The next morning Cantin, accompanied by two naturalist guides, unearthed the rest of the animal. It is the largest fossil ever found in the Escuminac Formation and arguably the most important one—a 1.57-meter-long complete skeleton of *Elpistostege*.

Seeing through Stone

Within days of Cantin's finding the fossil, Cloutier was invited to study it. Because most of the skeleton was still entombed in rock, the first order of business was to get a better look at it by using computed tomography (CT). Cloutier recruited Isabelle Béchard, one of his former master's students in paleontology, to help him image the specimen using a nonmedical CT scanner at the Institut National de la Recherche Scientifique (INRS) in Québec City. The scan showed that the specimen was absolutely complete—every single bone was preserved—but the resolution was not good enough to reveal the internal structure of the bones, which they wanted to be able to study. They had to find another CT scanner that provided better resolution. They decided that *Elpistostege* was going to travel some 3,900 kilometers south to the High-Resolution X-ray Computed Tomography Facility at the University of Texas at Austin, where each piece of the fossil would be scanned with the greatest precision available at the time.

Once the scanning was done, Cloutier and his colleagues began the meticulous work of preparing the fossil—removing the surrounding rock bit by bit to expose the bones within. They performed this work on a computer model of the fossil based on the CT scans as well as on the actual fossil. After a few months the body and the skull emerged from the rock, both virtually and in reality. The whole specimen was incredible, but the pectoral fins generated particular excitement because no one had ever seen a complete pectoral fin of an elpistostegalian before. Numerous skeletal elements were visible within the fins, surrounded by scales and fin rays. At first glance *Elpistostege*'s fin looked quite similar to that of *Tiktaalik*, but *Elpistostege*'s appeared to have additional bones in it. What were they?

In the years that followed, Cloutier and Béchard presented preliminary results of their analyses of the *Elpistostege* skeleton to colleagues at professional meetings. It was after one such presentation, in 2014 at the Society of Vertebrate Paleontology in Berlin, that Cloutier and one of us (Long) agreed over a beer to collaborate on the study of this remarkable fossil.

Long had been working on Devonian fish fossils from the Gogo Formation in Western Australia for many years. The skeletons of these ancient fishes are perfectly preserved in three dimensions, and some specimens show exceptional preservation of soft tissues as well. To study these fossils, which are found inside nodules of limestone, Long and his colleagues traditionally placed them in acid baths to dissolve the rock. More recently, they have shifted to imaging the fossils using CT and synchrotron scanners and sophisticated software to elucidate their fine anatomical structures before the acid baths, so that they can capture any soft-tissue preservation before the acid destroys it. The new *Elpistostege* specimen, with its exquisite preservation, seemed like a prime candidate for Long's approach to imaging and digital preparation.

In 2014 Long visited Cloutier's lab in Quebec and began working with his team on how to use different methods to process the imaging data from this fish. It took some trial and error with different types of data and software, but eventually we hit on a winning combination that would allow us to digitally isolate and study each bone. Alice Clement of Flinders University in Adelaide and Roxanne Noël and Vincent Roy, then master's students working under Cloutier, went on to carry out this work.

When Clement eventually began segmenting out the pectoral fin, we were at the edges of our seats. As the first complete elpistostegalian pectoral fin ever discovered, it was certain to contain vital clues to the transition from fins to limbs. The preliminary results did not disappoint. They not only confirmed Béchard's initial CT results suggesting the presence of extra bones in *Elpistostege*'s fin but also showed those bones in far greater detail. Now we could see that the fossil included an unexpected series of many small, tightly packed bones. Typically the end of the pectoral fin skeleton contains small bones called radials that support the rodlike fin rays. The bones evident in this part of *Elpistostege*'s fin were in the right place to be radials, but the large number of bones and the way some of them were arranged in discrete rows suggested that they were something else. We strongly suspected that these never-before-seen bones hidden in the pectoral fin of this ancient fish were actually digit bones similar to the ones found in the fingers of tetrapods. We identified two digits that were each composed of multiple, articulated bones, as well as three possible digits each composed of a single bone.

Why is the case for digit bones in the pectoral fins of *Elpistostege* more compelling than the earlier argument for digit bones in the pectoral fins of *Panderichthys*? The putative digit bones in *Panderichthys* are irregular in shape, and none of them show articulation with other bones in the standard way digit bones, or phalanges, do in the human hand. We surmise from comparison with the bones of the *Elpistostege* fin that the mystery bones in the *Panderichthys* pectoral fin are probably equivalent to some of the carpal bones in the wrists of tetrapods.

Fish out of Water

As the team finished isolating the entire pectoral fin and girdle such that every bone could be studied in every aspect, we also began segmenting out internal features of the skull and braincase. This work would help inform our understanding not only of *Elpistostege*'s anatomy but also of how it is related to other early fishes and to tetrapods.

To figure out where *Elpistostege* belongs in the family tree, we needed to compare it with other species, paying special attention to their shared distinctive features. Working with Mike Lee of Flinders, a leading expert on methods for ascertaining relations among species, we ran a phylogenetic analysis of 202 characteristics across 43 species. In the end, we were astounded to find that *Elpistostege* appears to be more closely related to the crown tetrapods—the group that includes all living tetrapods and their last common ancestor—than the well-known *Tiktaalik* is, though not by much. Our best guess is that the unique features of the pectoral fin, which is not fully preserved in *Tiktaalik*, plus some newly discovered features of the pectoral girdle (the bones that connect to the fins), pulled *Elpistostege* up a notch above *Tiktaalik* on the evolutionary ladder.

Combining what we see in the skeleton of *Elpistostege* with what the phylogenetic analysis tells us about its place in the family tree, we can reconstruct how the basic plan for the hands of tetrapods, including humans, originated. The presence of small rows of bones we identified as digits in the pectoral fin of *Elpistostege* shows that the arrangement first evolved in the fins of advanced lobe-finned fishes back at the start of the Late Devonian period, more than 380 million years ago. It is likely that they served to bear weight because having many tiny bones in alignment in this region would have given the outer part of the robust fin the flexibility needed to push the fish upward.

Why might a fish benefit from being able to maneuver in this way? The skull of *Elpistostege* contains a clue: at the back of the head is a pair of large holes called spiracles. Some modern-day fishes that breathe air have similarly large spiracles. For a long time, the function of these holes was uncertain. In a study published in 2014, Long worked with a team of ichthyologists at Scripps Institute of Oceanography in La Jolla, Calif., led by the late Jeff Graham, to nail it down. Analyzing the spiracles of the living bichir Polypterus, we showed that they are instrumental in breathing air. Assuming the spiracles served the same purpose in *Elpistostege*, the ability to employ the fins to do a push-up in the shallow rivers and estuary this fish inhabited—and thereby get the head out of water for a breath of fresh air—could have been advantageous.

Elpistostege was not necessarily restricted to the aquatic realm, however. Today's lungfish and some catfishes can propel themselves along land for short periods with their fins. With its far more powerfully built fins, *Elpistostege* was probably that much more capable of venturing ashore.

Baby Steps

In addition to upending the received wisdom about when fins became limbs, our discovery of digit bones in *Elpistostege* bears on efforts to understand the genetic and developmental changes that powered this transformation. Just a few decades ago scientists interested in this question did not have much to go on. Back then, there were only a few examples of fossil fishes with pectoral anatomy transitional between fins and limbs, and they hinted only that the arm and forearm bones evolved gradually. In contrast, it looked as though tetrapods evolved the hand and wrist from the ancestral fish fin all at once. But was it actually possible for such drastic change to occur so abruptly? Or was the seemingly sudden origin of the hand and wrist simply an artifact of an incomplete fossil record?

In a milestone paper published in 1991, the late developmental biologist Peter Thorogood proposed that the hand and wrist really could have originated quite suddenly. He based his proposal on comparisons of embryological development in fishes and tetrapods. In early-stage embryos of both groups, a structure called the apical ectodermal ridge (AER) acts as a signaling center that guides development of the fin and limb, respectively. Located in the tip of the budding fin and limb, the AER secretes chemicals that promote the outgrowth of the underlying tissue. In fish, the AER is active for only a short while before it transforms into another signaling center, the apical ectodermal fold (AEF), which directs the formation of the fin rays. In tetrapods, however, the AER is much more active in directing development because it persists far longer in the embryo–it does not ever morph into the AEF; thus, the fin rays do not form. So it has more time to develop the other bones of the appendage, which are the basis for making a hand. Thorogood suggested that the loss of the AER-AEF transition–a relatively simple tweak in the grand scheme of things–could produce both the loss of the fin rays and other characteristics of the pectoral fins and the simultaneous gain of the bones needed to form a wrist and digits.

The discovery of *Tiktaalik*, the first fossil fish to show not just the fish equivalent of our arm bones and some of the proximal wrist bones (those closest to the center of the body) but also bones from the distal part of the fin corresponding to our distal wrist bones, spurred research into the genetic and developmental underpinnings of the fin-to-limb transition. Investigators were keen to figure out which bones in the ancestral fish fin evolved into wrist and hand bones and which genes were responsible for generating that new morphology. Members of the *Hox* family of genes, which are well known to direct the different regions of the embryo to develop into the head, tail, and so forth, seemed likely to be involved.

In 2007 Zerina Johanson of the Natural History Museum in London and her colleagues studied the activity of one of these genes, *HoxD13*, in one of the closest living relatives of tetrapods, the Australian lungfish. Previous research had shown that *HoxD13* is active in the developing tetrapod limb when the wrists and digits form. Johanson's team showed that the gene is also active during the development of the radial bones in the lungfish fin. But whereas in tetrapod limb development *HoxD13* has two phases of activity–an early phase associated with the arm and forearm development and a late phase associated with wrist and digit development–it appears to have only one interval of activity in lungfish-fin development, corresponding to the second phase of the gene's activity in the developing tetrapod limb. The work suggested that tetrapod digit bones evolved from the radial bones in the fish fin. But wrist and hand could not have originated as a package deal, as Thorogood proposed, because lungfish and other living and fossil lobe-finned fishes have radials or wrist bones without having digits. There had to have been at least two evolutionary events, one that produced digits and another that produced wrists.

Elpistostege further complicates the story. It suggests that, contrary to Johanson's argument, the radials of lungfish and other lobe-finned fish are not all equivalent to digits. Instead only the most distal ones are homologous to digit bones; the proximal radials are homologous to the wrist bones and the long bones of the palm. What is more, *Elpistostege* reveals yet another step in the fin-limb transition. Because it preserves both wrist bones and digits, as well as fin rays, Elpistostege shows that loss of the fin rays must have been another, separate phase in the evolution of the hand.

The anatomical condition of the pectoral fins and digits we have described in *Elpistostege* suggests that we still need to fine-tune our understanding of the genetic and developmental mechanisms that drove their evolution. Nevertheless, with the entire skeleton preserved and many further studies of it underway, this specimen of *Elpistostege* seems destined to serve as a Rosetta Stone to solve the mystery of how limbs evolved from fins—and thus how vertebrates conquered land.

About the Authors

John A. Long is strategic professor in paleontology at Flinders University in South Australia. His research focuses on the early evolution of vertebrates, including the three-dimensionally preserved Devonian-age fossil fishes found in the Gogo formation in Western Australia. In 2020 he received the prestigious Bettison and James Award for lifelong achievement for his work as both a scientist and an author.

Richard Cloutier is a professor-researcher in evolutionary biology at the University of Québec at Rimouski. His research interests revolve around the evolutionary patterns and mechanisms of early vertebrates, as well as the evolutionary developmental biology of recent fishes and amphibians. He has been working on the fauna, paleoecology and paleoenvironment of the Devonian Miguasha fossil site for more than 30 years.

Fossils Upend Conventional Wisdom about Evolution of Human Bipedalism

By Jeremy DeSilva

Long before our ancestors evolved large brains and language, even before they tamed fire or made stone tools, they started doing something no mammal had done before: walking on two legs. Skeletal adaptations for traveling upright are evident in fossils of the very oldest hominins—members of the human family—which date to between seven million and five million years ago. Moving on two legs rather than four set the stage for subsequent evolutionary changes in our lineage. It allowed our predecessors to expand their home ranges and diversify their diets, and it transformed the way we give birth and parent our children. This peculiar mode of locomotion was foundational to virtually all the other characteristics that make humans unique.

In the iconic representation of human evolution, a procession of ancestors starting with a chimplike creature ambling on all fours gives way to a series of ever more erect forebears, culminating in a fully upright *Homo sapiens* striding triumphantly on two legs. First popularized in the 1960s, the March of Progress, as this image and its variants are known, has decorated countless books, T-shirts, bumper stickers and coffee mugs.

But paleoanthropological discoveries made over the past two decades are forcing scientists to redraw this traditional, linear imagery. We now know that various hominin species living in different environments throughout Africa, sometimes contemporaneously, evolved different ways to walk on two legs. The emergence of bipedalism kicked off a long phase of rampant evolutionary riffing on this form of locomotion. Our modern stride was not predetermined, with each successive ancestor marching closer to a particular end goal (evolution has no plans, after all). Rather it's one of many forms of upright walking that early hominins tried out—and the version that ultimately prevailed.

Mysterious Footprints

They didn't want to get hit by a flying lump of elephant poop. Who would? So paleontologists Kay Behrensmeyer and Andrew Hill, who were visiting archaeologist Mary Leakey's fossil site of Laetoli in Tanzania, hopped into a gully to take cover and gather more ammunition for the game of elephant dung dodgeball that had spontaneously broken out. It was July 24, 1976, the day of one of the most serendipitous discoveries in the history of paleoanthropology.

Hill and Behrensmeyer scanned the ground for dung but instead spotted fossilized elephant footprints and raindrop impressions hardened in an exposed layer of volcanic ash that fell 3.66 million years ago. A truce was called in the dung fight, and the others came to marvel at what had been found. Fossils speak broadly about an organism; fossil footprints capture precious snapshots of moments in time for long-extinct animals.

For the next few weeks Leakey and her team explored an area they called Site A, brushing aside overlying sediment to reveal thousands of footprints, mostly made by small antelopes and hares but also from ancient elephants, rhinoceroses, giraffes, large cats, birds and even a beetle. Hoping to find hominins in the mix, Leakey told the group to be on the lookout for bipedal footprints. Maybe they'd get lucky. That September they did. Peter Jones and Philip Leakey discovered five consecutive footprints made by something traveling on two, rather than four, legs. A hominin? Maybe, but the footprints were strangely shaped, and whatever made them had cross-stepped, moving the left foot over the right like a model on a runway rather than walking in the usual human way. The Site A bipedal trackway was a mystery.

Two years later two other members of Leakey's team, Paul Abell and Ndibo Mbuika, discovered another bipedal trackway two kilometers west of Site A at a location dubbed Site G. Two or three, perhaps even four, individuals had walked stride for stride through the muddy ash, leaving 69 stunningly humanlike footprints. Most scholars agree these tracks were made by *Australopithecus afarensis*—

Lucy's species–fossils of which have been found at Laetoli. The Site G tracks were decidedly different from the ones at Site A, however. If a hominin made the tracks at Site G, then what kind of creature made the bipedal trackway at Site A?

In the mid-1980s University of Chicago anthropologist Russ Tuttle took a crack at solving this mystery. After comparing the shape of the Site A footprints with those made by unshod humans, chimpanzees, and circus bears trained to walk on two legs, Tuttle concluded that the prints were either made by a second species of hominin that roamed Laetoli during the Pliocene epoch or made by a bipedally walking bear. Perhaps because a linear view of the evolution of human bipedalism was the dominant paradigm, other researchers embraced the bear hypothesis. As a result, whereas the Site G hominin footprints were exhaustively studied and became world-famous, the footprints at Site A fell into obscurity. Three decades passed before anyone focused on them again.

Dartmouth College, where I teach anthropology, is a small liberal arts school in New Hampshire nestled in a valley between that state's White Mountains and the Green Mountains of Vermont. Although the school is only two hours by car from metro Boston, its motto is *vox clamantis in deserto*, which translates to "a voice crying out in the wilderness." Large swaths of sugar maples provide an ample supply of syrup, the famous Appalachian Trail abuts the campus, and bears–a lot of bears–live in the surrounding woods.

In 2017 my then graduate student Ellison McNutt, who is now a professor of anatomy at Ohio University, and I teamed up with local black bear expert Ben Kilham to collect footprints from cubs whose feet were similar in size to the tracks at Laetoli Site A. Using maple syrup and applesauce to tempt them, we persuaded the young bears to rear up on their hind legs and amble through an experimental trackway filled with mud. To our surprise, their footprints and gait mechanics were no match for Site A. Bears' heel impressions are narrow, and their steps are widely spaced because their hip and knee anatomy causes them to wobble back and forth when walking bipedally. We started to have our doubts about the bear hypothesis.

More than 40 years have passed since the discovery of the Site A trackway. In that time, seasonal rains have slowly washed sediment from the barren hills at Laetoli, exposing tens of thousands of fossils. Teams led by Charles Musiba of the University of Colorado Denver, Terry Harrison of New York University and Denise Su of Arizona State University have recovered many of these fossils. We know from other sites that an extinct bear called *Agriotherium* did roam Africa during the Pliocene, but not one of the animal fossils these teams have recovered at Laetoli is from a bear. Someone needed to take another look at the bipedal tracks at Site A. But those same seasonal rains that gift us fossil bones and footprints also have the erosive power to take them away. We had assumed the Site A bipedal footprints were long gone. Thankfully, we were wrong.

In 2019 Musiba and I traveled to Laetoli and used Mary Leakey's detailed drawings like a treasure map to identify the precise location where the mysterious bipedal footprints should be. Then we began to dig. After several days Tanzanian team member Kallisti Fabian called to us, "*Mtu*"–the Swahili word for "human." He had found the footprints. The rains had not destroyed them but had covered and preserved all five of them with a layer of fine sediment. Using tongue depressors and thick-bristled brushes, we fully cleaned the prints, revealing never before seen details of the toe impressions, which we captured with high-resolution, 3-D laser scans unavailable to our colleagues working in the 1970s. The heel impressions of the Site A footprints are large, and the big toe is the dominant digit, as it is in humans and our ape cousins. This was no bear. A hominin made these tracks. But which hominin?

Walk on a sandy beach, and you are sure to see a variety of *H. sapiens* footprints–small, flat prints made by a toddler next to the long, arched prints of her mother, for instance. Modern humans come in all shapes and sizes, and so do our feet. Almost certainly, the same was also true for *A. afarensis*. Maybe the footprints at Sites A and G were showing normal variation within a single species of hominin. If so, the small size of the Site A footprints might indicate they were made by a child of Lucy's species. That's what I originally hypothesized, anyway.

Footprint expert Kevin Hatala of Chatham University, who helped to discover and analyze 1.55-million-year-old *Homo erectus* footprints at Ileret, Kenya, joined our team, and together we compared the shape of the Site A footprints with the best-preserved footprints from Site G and another trackway discovered in 2015 at Site S, along with hundreds of footprints made by humans and chimpanzees. The differences we observed did not fit within the range of variation among footprints from people of all ages today.

We found that the Site A footprints had a shape that was as different from the Site G and S prints as a chimpanzee's footprints are from yours and mine. That's not to say the Site A footprints were just like a chimpanzee's, only that they were very different in shape from those of Lucy's species. Compared with those presumed *A. afarensis* footprints at Sites G and S, the Site A footprints were short and wide, the big toe stuck out to the side a bit, and there was some evidence the walkers had a more flexible middle portion of the foot.

In our paper describing these findings, published in the journal *Nature*, we claimed that not only were the Site A footprints from a hominin, but they also were evidence of a second species at Laetoli. As is expected in science, not all of our colleagues have fully embraced our interpretation. Some think we just found another *A. afarensis* footprint trail. But it is worth repeating that the Site A footprints were so different from the Site G *Australopithecus* prints that our field was convinced for decades that they were made by a bear.

It seems to me that shortly after ash fell from the sky 3.66 million years ago, two kinds of hominins, walking on slightly different feet in slightly different ways, moved north toward the Olduvai Basin in Tanzania, perhaps in search of water. Because it is thought that the footprint layer at Laetoli captures at most a few days of activity, this is the best evidence we have that different Pliocene hominin species not only were contemporaries but shared the same landscape. How they interacted—if at all—is anyone's guess at this point.

Fossil Feet

The rediscovery of the Laetoli Site A footprints and our conclusion that they were made by a second species are the latest additions to a growing body of evidence that the evolution of upright walking was a lot less linear, more complex and more interesting than we once thought. The other evidence comes not from footprints but from fossils of the hominins themselves. Isolated foot bones are rare in the human fossil record, and foot skeletons are even more elusive. So it is exciting that in the past two decades, paleoanthropologists searching in Africa's Great Rift Valley and in caves in South Africa have quadrupled the number of fossils from the only part of a biped's body usually in direct contact with the ground. Many of these new discoveries sample a pivotal period in human evolution, between five million and three million years ago, when our ancestors were becoming committed upright walkers. In 2017 McNutt and I teamed up with Bernhard Zipfel, a former podiatrist-turned paleoanthropologist at the University of the Witwatersrand in South Africa, to make sense of these finds.

Specifically, we sought to evaluate the received wisdom about the evolution of bipedalism in light of the new fossil evidence. According to the traditional view, hominins started out with a chimplike foot built for grasping tree branches. This foot evolved into a transitional foot capable of both grasping and walking, as seen in the fossil known as Ardi, a member of *Ardipithecus ramidus* that lived in Aramis, Ethiopia, 4.4 million years ago. Fast forward to Lucy, the *A. afarensis* individual who lived in Hadar, Ethiopia, some 3.2 million years ago, whose foot has a big heel and a stiff midfoot that were better adapted to life on the ground. With the emergence of our own genus, *Homo*, roughly a million years later, the foot became even better suited to terrestrial locomotion, evolving shorter toes and a high arch.

After studying all the foot fossils carefully curated in museums throughout Africa, we noticed a very different pattern emerging from our data. As bipedalism evolved in our earliest ancestors, there was a burst of evolutionary experimentation that resulted in different hominins having different foot forms. We identified five different foot morphs, possibly indicating five distinct ways of walking upright, in the two-million-year interval we studied. Between the chronological bookends of Ardi and Lucy are three other uniquely shaped feet. The first belongs to an Ardi-type creature, about the same age as that fossil, from Gona, Ethiopia; the second comes from a 3.67-million-year-old hominin from Sterkfontein, South Africa, dubbed "Little Foot"; and the third is a strikingly primitive foot from a site called Burtele in Woranso-Mille, Ethiopia, that dates to 3.4 million years ago. Although all five of these hominin feet exhibit both apelike and humanlike features, these traits occur in a completely different combination in each foot and do not follow the predicted pattern of becoming less apelike and more humanlike over time.

Like an ancient version of the story of Cinderella, perhaps one of these recently discovered feet will fit the mysterious hominin footprints at Laetoli Site A and reveal the identity of the track maker. We'll see as we continue to explore these early stages of our evolutionary history.

Sustained Diversity

Intriguingly, the pattern of locomotor diversity is not limited to these early chapters of human evolution. Take, for instance, *Australopithecus sediba*. Rivaling the elephant dung fight in the lore of fortuitous paleoanthropological discoveries, this nearly two-million-year-old hominin was discovered in 2008 by then nine-year-old Matthew Berger. He literally stumbled over a rock containing a hominin clavicle and lower jaw while surveying for fossils at the site of Malapa Cave in South Africa's Cradle of Humankind with his father, paleoanthropologist Lee Berger of the University of the Witwatersrand. In the months that followed, Berger and his team excavated the fossil-bearing cave walls and discovered two partial skeletons of a new species they called *A. sediba*. Berger invited me to study the foot and leg fossils shortly after I had completed my Ph.D.

I was shocked by what I saw. The shapes of the bones were all wrong. For a hominin of this time period, the heel bone was too apelike, and the midfoot, ankle, knee, hip and lower back showed strange traits in both skeletons. In isolation, these bones were bizarre. But in concert, they told the story of a hominin with a peculiar way of walking, one that was similar to that of humans today who hyperpronate, or excessively transfer weight to the inside of their foot. This gait can lead to joint pathologies in modern people, but Berger and I and our colleagues interpreted the peculiarly shaped bones of *A. sediba* as anatomical solutions to the problems modern humans face when they walk in this manner. In other words, we think this species was adapted to walk in this way. Why? The shoulders and arms of *A. sediba* indicate that it climbed trees, and its teeth preserve microscopic traces of plant cells derived from leaves, fruit and bark—evidence that this species frequently fed in trees. This way of walking was the compromise for a hominin well adapted for life in two worlds, navigating between the trees and the ground—long after other hominin species had fully committed to terrestrial life.

A. sediba was not the only hominin walking around southern Africa two million years ago. In 2020 a team of researchers led by Andy Herries of La Trobe University in Australia reported newly discovered fossils from the Drimolen Cave system, also in the Cradle of Humankind area. These fossils came from two other hominin species: the large-toothed *Paranthropus robustus* and the much more humanlike *H. erectus*. In other words, three different kinds of hominins from three different genera—*Homo, Paranthropus*, and *Australopithecus*—were coexisting.

We know from a partial skeleton discovered in the 1980s along the western side of Lake Turkana in Kenya that *H. erectus* had a body form nearly identical to that of humans living today. Footprints on the eastern side of the lake confirm that these hominins walked like us. *H. erectus*—the likely ancestor to the lineage that led to our own species, *H. sapiens*—would have peered across its territory and seen two other bipeds from two different genera, *Australopithecus* and *Paranthropus*. Given the different shapes of their foot and leg bones, I think these hominins all had different styles of walking.

The pattern of diverse walking styles persisted even after *Australopithecus* and *Paranthropus* went extinct. As recently as 60,000 years ago, by which point *H. sapiens* was well established, the small human species *Homo floresiensis*, nicknamed the Hobbit, roamed its island home of Flores in Indonesia on relatively giant, flat feet and short legs with small joints. I wonder if the resulting gait would include the short steps and high knee drive of a person in snowshoes.

Perhaps gait differences helped hominins determine whether a group foraging in the distance belonged to their own species or another. And if gait did reveal the distant foragers to be from their same species, could the observers tell whether the other individuals were friends and family or strangers? Knowing the answer could have been the difference between avoiding conflict and inviting it. Gait, it turns out, is more than a means of getting from point A to point B.

Open Questions

Many questions remain about the evolution of bipedalism. We still do not know why upright walking was selectively advantageous for our earliest ancestors and extinct relatives. Hypotheses abound. In 1809 French naturalist Jean-Baptiste Lamarck speculated that humans evolved upright walking to see over tall grass. Six decades later Charles Darwin surmised that walking on two legs freed the hands to use tools. Other scholars have since proposed that it allowed our ancestors to gather and carry food or to wade through shallow water. Still others argue that it offered a more energetically efficient means of traveling between scattered resources. It seems to me, though, that efforts to identify *the* reason bipedalism evolved are a fool's errand. Instead I think it's possible–maybe even probable–that bipedalism evolved multiple times at the base of the hominin family tree, perhaps for different reasons, in different hominins living in slightly different environments throughout Africa. The diversity of foot forms found in Pliocene fossil sites across the continent supports such a scenario.

The fossil record of apes from the Miocene epoch (23 million to 5.3 million years ago) highlights other unknowns. Paleoanthropologists working in Africa have struggled to find ape fossils from this all-important time period when hominins diverged from other apes. But their counterparts in southern Europe have turned up an impressive collection of bones from apes that used to live in Spain, France, Germany, Greece, Italy, Hungary and Turkey. Judging from their hands, arms, backs, hips and legs, these European apes didn't knuckle-walk like a chimpanzee. Instead some of them may have been able to move on two legs more often and more efficiently than modern African apes do. Depending on where these ancient apes—such as the 11.6-million-year-old *Danuvius guggenmosi* from Germany, first announced in 2019—fit into the family tree, it is even possible that the ape from which the ancestors of humans, chimpanzees and gorillas split was not a knuckle-walker at all but more upright, using hand-assisted bipedalism to "walk" through the trees. In that case, the unique hominin adaptation would be not bipedal walking per se but rather bipedal walking *on the ground*. If more fossils continue to support this hypothesis, then rudimentary bipedalism might turn out not to be a new form of locomotion at all; it may be an old one co-opted for a new environment as our ancestors shifted from an arboreal to a terrestrial existence.

This idea is controversial and in need of further testing. The challenge is that paleoanthropologists have yet to unearth fossil foot or leg bones from Africa during the key time period when the lineages that would eventually lead to humans, chimpanzees and gorillas were beginning to diverge, between 12 million and seven million years ago. To fill in that gap, we rely on the anatomy of those ancient apes from southern Europe. In a way, it is like trying to figure out what your great-grandmother looked like by studying tattered black-and-white photographs of your 19th-century cousins three times removed. They'll provide some clues but not the full picture.

We'll see how this hypothesis holds up in the decades to come as more fossils are recovered from sites around the Mediterranean and in Africa. For now, though, the very beginnings of upright walking remain shrouded in mystery.

Once our ancestors got moving on two legs, they kept on walking, and that journey has continued right up to today. In a lifetime, the average person will take about 150 million steps—enough to circle Earth three times. We stroll, stride, plod, traipse, amble, saunter, shuffle, tiptoe, lumber, tromp, lope, strut and swagger. After walking all over someone, we might be asked to walk a mile in their shoes. Heroes walk on water, and geniuses are walking encyclopedias. But rarely do we humans *think* about walking. It has become, you might say, pedestrian. The fossils, however, reveal something else entirely. Walking is anything but ordinary. Instead it is a complex, convoluted evolutionary experiment that began with humble apes taking their first steps in Miocene forests and eventually set hominins on a path around the world.

About the Author

Jeremy DeSilva is a paleoanthropologist at Dartmouth College. His research focuses on the evolution of bipedalism. He is author of First Steps: How Upright Walking Made Us Human *(HarperCollins, 2021).*

Rockshelter Discoveries Show Neandertals Were a Lot like Us

By David W. Frayer and Davorka Radovcic

In March 2021, as Texas and Mississippi lifted their coronavirus pandemic mask mandates against the advice of health officials, President Joe Biden accused the governors of those states of "Neandertal thinking." Biden was right to be concerned about rolling back coronavirus restrictions too soon, but he was wrong to use our evolutionary cousins as the basis for his reprimand.

Biden is hardly alone in wielding "Neandertal" as a pejorative term. In popular culture, it is common to make fun of Neandertals, pointing to their primitive physical features, their backward ways, their overall stupidity. Merriam-Webster suggests "clod," "lout" and "oaf" as suitable synonyms for "Neandertal." Even some of our paleoanthropologist colleagues consider Neandertals–who ruled Eurasia from 350,000 to 30,000 years ago–less than human, deficient in many of the cognitive and behavioral abilities typical of our kind.

Yet numerous studies underscore the similarities between Neandertals and us. Finds at Neandertal sites across Eurasia show that they had innovative technology, complex foraging strategies and nascent symbolic traditions.

Not everyone is convinced. Critics have argued that Neandertals learned advanced behaviors or acquired fancy goods from the modern humans they encountered rather than developing them independently.

Our research on Neandertal material from the site of Krapina in northwestern Croatia over the past 15 years provides evidence that the critics are wrong. The Neandertals there exhibited a range of behaviors traditionally assumed to be unique to modern humans, and they developed these behaviors independently, tens of thousands of years before modern humans arrived in this region. Much remains to be discovered about these enigmatic members of the human family, but it is now abundantly clear that they were behaving in cognitively sophisticated ways long before they ever met up with the likes of us.

The Original Others

The Neandertals' bad rap traces back to the mid-1800s, when British geologist William King wrote of the skull of the first Neandertal fossil from Germany: "the thoughts and desires which once dwelt within it never soared beyond those of the brute." This perception of Neandertals gained currency in the early 1900s, when French anatomist Marcellin Boule reconstructed a Neandertal skeleton from the site of La Chapelle-aux-Saints in France as a stooped, apelike creature–one that he saw as primitive in body and therefore mind. Ever since, paleoanthropologists have been debating just how much like us the Neandertals were in terms of anatomy as well as behavior.

For a long time it looked as though Neandertal behavior differed from that of early modern humans in several important respects. Researchers argued that Neandertals had the same tool kit for tens of thousands of years, whereas early modern humans eventually went on to make a variety of more complex tools that used a wider range of raw materials and took more steps to create. Similarly, moderns appeared to eat a far more varied diet of animal and plant foods compared with the Neandertals' apparent focus on large game. And moderns seemed to be unique in developing art and rituals.

In recent years, though, paleoanthropologists have recovered evidence of Neandertals behaving in ways no one would have predicted just a couple of decades ago. Bruce Hardy and his colleagues have found bits of ancient twisted thread at the site of Abris du Maras in France that show Neandertals had fiber technology. Marie Soressi and her collaborators discovered specialized bone tools called lissoirs, which are used for leatherworking, at Pech-de-l'Azé rockshelter in France. João Zilhão and his team have shown that Neandertals were eating mussels, crabs, sharks and seals, among other marine resources, at Figueira Brava in Portugal and other coastal sites. Elsewhere in Europe researchers have found indications that Neandertals exploited a wide variety of plant foods and even mushrooms.

It is not just previously unknown Neandertal technology and dietary strategies that have come to light. Other discoveries demonstrate that Neandertals engaged in symbolic behaviors, such as decorating their bodies and making art. Marco Peresani and his group have reported on cut marks on bird wings found in Fumane Cave in Italy that indicate Neandertals were collecting feathers. A team led by Clive Finlayson uncovered an abstract image resembling a hashtag etched into the floor of Gorham's Cave in Gibraltar. Dirk Leder and his colleagues found a toe bone from a giant deer engraved with a geometric pattern at the site of Einhornhöhle in Germany.

Researchers have unearthed many such examples of Neandertal creativity. But controversy has often accompanied their claims. Most evidence of Neandertal symbolism dates to the latter part of the Neandertals' reign, by which point anatomically modern humans were beginning to filter into Europe. Perhaps, critics have suggested, Neandertals merely copied what moderns were doing or obtained symbolic items from them through trade or even theft. Alternatively, at cave sites that were inhabited at different times by both groups, maybe natural disturbances–such as moving water or denning animals–mixed modern goods in with Neandertal remains. What investigators needed to find to bolster their case for Neandertal sophistication was evidence of advanced Neandertal behavior that was substantially older than the earliest-known modern humans in Europe. This is where our work at Krapina comes in.

Symbolic Behavior

From 1899 to 1905 Croatian paleontologist Dragutin Gorjanović-Kramberger directed excavations at the Krapina rockshelter, collecting some 900 Neandertal bones, nearly 200 isolated Neandertal teeth, and thousands of animal bones and stone tools. He was a meticulous excavator. Uncommonly for his era, he dug in levels–removing one horizontal layer of sediment, bones and artifacts at a time–and saved much of what he excavated. In 1906 Gorjanović-Kramberger published a comprehensive monograph on the bones and tools from the site. To this day, Krapina remains one of Europe's richest Neandertal sites; thousands of publications about its inhabitants have appeared since 1899.

Our recent research provides unexpected new insights into the Neandertals who lived and died at Krapina some 130,000 years ago. In 2013 one of us (Radovčić) did a complete inventory of all the material from the site and "rediscovered" some unusual white-tailed eagle remains–eight talons and a foot bone–whose importance had previously gone unappreciated. Each bore multiple signs of having been intentionally modified. Discovered in the uppermost level at the site, the talons and foot bone were found in the same sedimentary layer as many cave bear bones, Neandertal tools, a fragmentary child's cranium and at least one hearth. No modern humans or modern tools are found at Krapina, so there is no doubt these white-tailed eagle bones are associated with Neandertals.

In life, eagle talons are covered with a thick carapace, which must have been stripped off, given the subsequent modifications on all the Krapina talons. One talon has cut marks on its upper surface and a preserved sinew fiber under a natural silicate coating, along with microscopic bits of red and yellow ochre in the pores on its surface. Three of the other Krapina talons and the phalanx show cut marks. The edges of many of these marks are eroded, which we think may be the result of the talons having been tied together with a binding such as sinew. Other marks, including notches cut into some of the talons, support the hypothesis that these talons were strung into some kind of ornamental object–probably a necklace or bracelet or perhaps a rattle.

We know from the duplication of right second talons in this assemblage that the eight talons and foot bone came from at least three different white-tailed eagles. In the Paleolithic, as in modern times, eagles were the largest aerial predators around. Their rarity in the landscape would have made them difficult prey to catch. It therefore seems unlikely this was a random collection of eagle feet.

Instead these remains signal that the Krapina Neandertals had some kind of specialized hunting strategy. Although single talons have turned up at other Neandertal sites and probably served as pendants, no other Neandertal site has yielded eight talons from the same archaeological level.

The eagle talons are not the only sign of symbolic behavior among the Krapina Neandertals. The site has also yielded a unique rock with starburstlike inclusions that went undescribed until Radovčić noticed it while inventorying the collection. Formed of mudstone dating to the Middle Triassic epoch, the rock could not have originated in the Krapina rockshelter, which is composed of sandstone. Rather it seems that a Neandertal collected it from nearby outcrops of rock to the north of the site. Measuring 92 by 66 millimeters, with a maximum thickness of 17 millimeters, it easily fits in the hand. Because it shows no signs of surface modification or use wear, we can be fairly certain it was not used as a tool.

The rock is remarkable for its numerous dendritic structures, which are exposed in cross section and longitudinally. The structures have a three-dimensional appearance and are especially brilliant when the piece is wet, which increases the contrast between the striking black branching structures and the brown cortex. At the bottom of the rock a long, curved black feature traverses the entire lower face with a concentration of dendritic forms in the midpoint. It is apparently the impression of some kind of fossilized plant stem.

Any modern-day rockhound would collect a rock like this one. Did a Krapina Neandertal experience that same feeling of wonder about this uniquely patterned stone when she or he picked it up? In any case, the object generated enough interest that its discoverer brought it home. The collection and curation of this stone show that Neandertals had an eye for aesthetically pleasing objects and assigned significance to them.

A partial Neandertal cranium from the site, known as Krapina 3, provides a different kind of evidence for symbolic behavior.

Assessed as a female based on its size and comparatively delicate build, the specimen bears 35 mostly parallel striations that run up the forehead. The marks show no signs of healing, so we know they were made after death. Other Neandertal bones from Krapina exhibit cut marks associated with defleshing related to cannibalism. But the cut marks on Krapina 3 are evenly spaced and differ from the closely packed criss-crossing butchering marks on these other specimens from the site. Nor do the cut marks appear to be the result of trampling of the bones by animals, which would have left more randomly scattered, overlapping marks.

Sometimes when anthropologists measure bones with calipers, the instrument can leave marks on the bone. But none of the standard measurements anthropologists take on skulls involve this part of the forehead. What is more, we know the cut marks are old because they are filled with cave sediment that buried the bone and are covered with lacquer, which paleontologists used to apply to fossils to preserve them. All these factors strongly suggest that a Neandertal made the marks.

Researchers have observed linear marks on bones at a few other Neandertal sites, but so far these cases involve only limb bones from animals found at these locales. The marks on the Krapina 3 Neandertal skull deviate from all the other examples of bone modification at the site and are unique in the fossil record. They probably signify some kind of ritual behavior, whether ceremonial modification of the remains of a loved one, numerical recording or doodling. Whatever the exact symbolic significance of these cut marks, the eagle talons or the starry stone, Neandertals were ascribing meaning to them 130,000 years ago–90,000 years before modern humans reached Croatia.

Righties and Lefties

Another symbolic behavior–one that scholars have often held up as a defining characteristic of modern humans and the secret of our success as a species–is language. Did Neandertals have language?

Did they gossip about their neighbors, talk about their hopes and fears, tell their children bedtime stories? Without a time machine to transport us back to their era, we cannot know for certain. But there are hints in the archaeological and fossil records. A number of archaeologists consider body ornaments and other physical manifestations of symbolism to be proxies for language. Neandertal fossils themselves also contain clues.

We set out to determine whether Neandertals preferentially used one hand over the other in their daily tasks. Right-handedness is a common human trait; right-handers dominate left-handers in every living human population. Handedness reflects the fact that the two hemispheres of the brain are asymmetrical, with each side specialized for different tasks. This brain lateralization, as it is termed, is associated with language capacity. Other primates exhibit varying degrees of lateralization, but only humans show such a high frequency of right-handedness.

To assess the handedness of the Krapina Neandertals, we used optical and scanning electron microscopy to examine scratches in the enamel of their incisor and canine teeth. These striations, which occur exclusively on the lip side of the teeth, were produced when a stone tool accidentally etched the enamel. This kind of damage can occur when an individual uses his or her teeth as a third hand of sorts to grip an object–for instance, an animal hide. When a right-hander holds a tool and rakes it across material held between the front teeth, as one might do to clean an animal hide, any time the tool hits a tooth, it will leave a right-angled scratch on the tooth. A left-hander leaves an oppositely angled scratch. By studying the angles of the scratch marks evident in even a single fossil tooth, we can determine whether it belonged to a right-handed or left-handed individual.

Our analysis of the Krapina Neandertal teeth identified nine right-handers and two left-handers. If we expand our sample to include Neandertals from other European sites, the ratio of right-handers to left-handers replicates the typical 9:1 pattern of living humans. Interestingly, this pronounced dominance of right-handedness is not found first in Neandertals but extends back to their European predecessors and an even earlier member of our genus, *Homo*, from Africa. Apparently hemispheric brain asymmetry—and thus perhaps language—is an ancient human trait.

Neandertals had more than just behavior in common with modern humans. In-depth studies at Krapina and other sites show that many morphological characteristics once thought to be unique to Neandertals are found in moderns, and some modern features are found in Neandertals. One such trait is the form of an opening on the tongue side of the lower jaw (mandible) called the mandibular foramen. The mandibular nerve passes through this opening to innervate the teeth, gums and chin. In modern humans, the upper portion of the foramen is commonly V-shaped. In most Neandertals, the opening is covered by a bar of bone and is called a horizontal-oval (H-O) foramen. But at Krapina, only four of the nine Neandertal mandibles that preserve this part of the bone have the typical Neandertal H-O foramen; five show the modern V-shaped pattern.

Numerous other cranial and postcranial features in the Krapina Neandertals overlap with early modern humans, too. No doubt Neandertals had a distinctive morphology, but many of their traits are also found much later in the modern people who followed them. It is very unlikely moderns independently evolved these Neandertal-like traits. Rather there was probably a lot of variation in Neandertal morphology, and in later times some interbreeding occurred between them and our modern European ancestors. The "unique" traits were passed on as part of these interbreeding events. Given the apparent cognitive similarities between Neandertals and early modern humans, we should perhaps not be surprised that the two groups saw each other as humans and exchanged genes when they encountered each other.

Despite the fact that excavations at Krapina were concluded more than a century ago, the stones and bones from the site continue to provide new information about Neandertals and their place in human evolution. Undoubtedly more secrets remain to be revealed in the Krapina collection. We are endeavoring to tease out some of them. For example, with colleagues from England and Italy, we have been obtaining high-resolution, synchrotron images of baby teeth from the site to evaluate growth rates as measured by enamel formation. Modern humans are unique among living primates in having an extended period of childhood growth, which gives our large, powerful brains time to develop. Researchers have debated just how similar Neandertal childhood development was to that of moderns'. Our results show that Neandertal infants formed their enamel a little faster than moderns, indicating a more rapid growth rate on average. Yet it was still in the modern range.

Mounting evidence from sites across Europe is forcing scientists to rethink their conception of these long-disparaged members of the human family. The Krapina Neandertals are an important part of this shift. We suspect that future discoveries at Krapina and beyond will further narrow the list of behavioral and anatomical traits that supposedly set Neandertals apart from moderns. They were not the same as us. But we have far more in common with them than not.

This article is dedicated to the memory of Jakov Radovčić, who served as curator of the Krapina Neandertal Collection for 32 years.

About the Authors

David W. Frayer is an emeritus professor of biological anthropology at the University of Kansas. He has studied skeletal variation and behavior in Neandertals and other early human populations spanning more than a million years.

Davorka Radovčić is curator of the Krapina Neandertal Collection at the Croatian Natural History Museum. Her research focuses on Neandertals, early modern humans and Homo naledi.

Mind Your "Fs" and "Vs": Agriculture May Have Shaped Both Human Jaws and Language

By Anne Pycha

The organs of speech are the same for all people, or so linguists have typically assumed. But it turns out that may not be true—in fact, what you eat can change how you talk.

The conventional wisdom held in the field of historical linguistics is the vocal apparatus of human beings has remained fixed since the emergence of *Homo sapiens* some 200,000 years ago. As a consequence, all humans, both ancient and modern peoples, possess the same basic capacity to produce speech sounds. But recent evidence from several studies in paleoanthropology has upended these assumptions by suggesting the way we eat can actually alter jaw anatomy. And according to research just published in *Science*, the consequences for the way we speak have been profound.

The lead authors of the study, Damián Blasi and Steven Moran of the University of Zurich along with colleagues, became intrigued by fossil evidence showing the form of the human jaw had changed in our species's relatively recent evolutionary past. Among hunter-gatherers of the Paleolithic period, adults' upper and lower teeth aligned to form a flat line, the top ones resting directly on the bottom set. Scientists attribute that configuration primarily to tooth wear brought about by chewing hard foods, such as unmilled grains or seeds. With the advent of agriculture in the post-Neolithic period, however, the upper teeth protruded over and above the lower teeth, presumably due to the reduced challenge of consuming soft foods such as porridge and cheese.

These findings suggest not only that the cultural shift that gave rise to agriculture occasioned a shift in human anatomy. It also appears to have introduced new speech sounds known as labiodentals—the "f" and "v," for instance. Blasi and Moran's study furnishes evidence that adopting the signature foodstuffs of sedentary society ultimately allowed us to mouth words like "farro" and "verbalize" by raising the lower lip and bringing it into contact with the upper teeth. Their research group conducted biomechanical simulations of this movement using two different virtual jaws to calculate the muscular effort involved. Their results showed, compared with the protruding bites, the flat bite configurations required substantially more effort to produce a labiodental.

Linguists had already established that articulatory effort can affect the fate of a phoneme, so Blasi and Moran's team speculated that labiodentals would have been less likely to emerge among any population with flat bites, such as Paleolithic humans, or even modern humans who eat harder foods. To test this hypothesis, they analyzed databases of the world's consonants and showed contemporary hunter–gatherer languages contain only a fraction of the labiodental sounds that food-producer languages do. Of course, food preparation techniques are merely a stand-in for actual bite configurations. To make the link more explicit, the researchers separately analyzed hunter–gatherer societies in Greenland, southern Africa and Australia, where flat bites have been explicitly documented. In line with their hypothesis, results turned up relatively few languages with labiodentals among these populations. When one of these sounds appeared, it was usually borrowed from other languages.

As a final piece of support for their argument, Blasi and Moran's team examined sound changes in Indo-European languages over time. They used a nontraditional technique called stochastic character mapping, which calculates the numerical probability a sound existed in a language at a particular point in time. Results showed labiodental sounds were extremely unlikely in almost all branches of Indo-European, until anytime from 6,000 to 4,000 years ago. After that period, which coincides with the introduction of soft foods, the probability of these sounds showed a notable increase.

The take-home message: "we can't take for granted that spoken languages sound the same today as they did in the distant past,"

Moran says. "This means in particular that the set of speech sounds we use has not necessarily remained stable since the emergence of our species, but rather the immense diversity of speech sounds that we find today is the product of a complex interplay of factors involving biological change and cultural evolution."

Not everyone is convinced of the arguments put forth in the new study. Israel Hershkovitz of Tel Aviv University points out many factors besides tooth wear can affect bite configurations. Also, tooth wear occurs gradually and does not fully affect bite dynamics until adulthood. Given the relatively short life expectancy of prehistoric hunter–gatherers, he says, it seems unlikely this anatomical trait could have affected language evolution.

To other observers, Blasi and Moran's study, along with others in recent years, reflects a paradigm shift in historical linguistics. "This paper revives an idea that linguists probably abandoned out of a natural apprehension—the danger of verging on ideas that could be interpreted as racist—which arises whenever anatomical differences between populations are proposed to play a role in any aspect of language or cognition," says Andrew Garrett of the University of California, Berkeley, who was not involved in the study. "Today, however, there is clear evidence that individual anatomical, physiological and perceptual differences do play some role in linguistic differences."

GLOSSARY

establishment clause The portion of the First Amendment to the U.S. Constitution that states that "Congress shall make no law respecting an establishment of religion."

fundamentalism A belief that the literal meaning of a religion's sacred text should be the basis of morality and teaching.

hierarchy A ranking of people according to a certain set of conditions, such as wealth, gender, or ethnicity.

ideology A coherent set of beliefs, often shared by community or culture.

intelligent design A form of creationism that claims that life on Earth was created by an intelligent being.

natural selection The process by which species survive and reproduce based on their ability to adapt to their environment.

paleontologist A scientist who studies past geological periods.

theory In science, a theory is an explanation of observable facts that can be and has been repeatedly tested and confirmed according to the scientific method.

uniformitarianism The scientific theory that Earth's major geological features were caused by the very slow accumulation of small changes.

FURTHER INFORMATION

Bai, Nina. "The Education of Jennifer Miller: An Update from the Frontline in the Fight against the Anti-Evolution Agenda," *Scientific American*, February 28, 2011, https://www.scientificamerican.com/article/the-education-of-jennifer-miller/.

Black, Riley. "New Evidence Emerges in Mystery of When Mammals Became Warm-Blooded," *Scientific American*, July 20, 2022, https://www.scientificamerican.com/article/new-evidence-emerges-in-mystery-of-when-mammals-became-warm-blooded./

Callier, Viviane. "Heated Debate Persists over the Origins of Complex Cells," *Scientific American*, June 13, 2022, https://www.scientificamerican.com/article/heated-debate-persists-over-the-origins-of-complex-cells/.

Golembiewski, Kate. "How Chewing Shaped Human Evolution," *New York Times*, August 17, 2022, https://www.nytimes.com/2022/08/17/science/chewing-human-evolution.html.

Harmon, Katherine. "Evolution Abroad: Creationism Evolves in Science Classrooms around the Globe," *Scientific American*, March 3, 2011, https://www.scientificamerican.com/article/evolution-education-abroad/.

Hunter, Dana. "Adventures in Creationist Earth Science Education: In the Beginning...," *Scientific American*, September 25, 2014. https://blogs.scientificamerican.com/rosetta-stones/adventures-in-creationist-earth-science-education-in-the-beginning-8230/.

Otto, Shawn Lawrence. "Antiscience Beliefs Jeopardize U.S. Democracy," *Scientific American*, November 1, 2012, https://www.scientificamerican.com/article/antiscience-beliefs-jeopardize-us-democracy/.

CITATIONS

1.1 When Lord Kelvin Nearly Killed Darwin's Theory by Mano Singham (September 5, 2021); 1.2 The Denialist Playbook by Sean B. Carroll (November 8, 2020); 1.3 On "Darwinism" by Kenneth Miller (April 17, 2018); 1.4 Book Review: God's Word or Human Reason? An Inside Perspective on Creationism by Darren Naish (March 25, 2018); 1.5 Science Denial versus Science Pleasure by Michael Shermer (January 1, 2018); 1.6 Denial of Evolution Is a Form of White Supremacy by Allison Hopper (July 5, 2021); 1.7 Scientists Should Admit They Bring Personal Values to Their Work by Naomi Oreskes (April 1, 2021); 2.1 50 Years Ago: Repeal of Tennessee's "Monkey Law" by Glenn Branch and Ann Reid (May 10, 2017); 2.2 Dissent with Modification: Soothing Evolution–Religion Tensions in the Classroom by Robin Lloyd (April 6, 2017); 2.3 Teachers Help One Another Bring Evolution Back to the Classroom by Adam Piore (August 1, 2018); 2.4 Evolution Is Still True, but... by Glenn Branch (November 26, 2018); 2.5 Evolution Education in the U.S. Is Getting Better by Glenn Branch and Ann Reid (September 12, 2020); 2.6 Science Education Is Under Legislative Attack by Glenn Branch (September 27, 2019); 3.1 That Mouse in Your House–It's Smarter, Thanks to You by Christopher Intagliata (March 9, 2021); 3.2 The Mangrove Finch: An Extinction in Slow Motion by John R. Platt (October 19, 2016); 3.3 Humans Make Wild Animals Less Wary by Jason G. Goldman (October 16, 2020); 3.4 Malaria Mosquitoes Are Biting before Bed-Net Time by Jason G. Goldman (May 21, 2020); 4.1 The Noninevitability of Life by Caleb A. Scharf (February 28, 2020); 4.2 The First Gene on Earth May Have Been a Hybrid by Andy Extance (June 22, 2020); 4.3 New Clues about the Origins of Biological Intelligence by Rafael Yuste and Michael Levin (December 11, 2021); 4.4 Evolution's Favorite Fish Diversify through 'Noncoding' Genes by Jason G. Goldman (May 1, 2021); 4.5 Fossils Reveal When Animals Started Making Noise by Michael B. Habib (January 1, 2022); 5.1 How Scientists Discovered the Staggering Complexity of Human Evolution by Kate Wong (September 1, 2020); 5.2 How a 380-Million-Year-Old Fish Gave Us Fingers by John A. Long and Richard Cloutier (June 1, 2020); 5.3 Fossils Upend Conventional Wisdom about Evolution of Human Bipedalism by Jeremy DeSilva (November 1, 2022); 5.4 Rockshelter Discoveries Show Neandertals Were a Lot like Us by David W. Frayer and Davorka Radovcic (February 1, 2022); 5.5 Mind Your "Fs" and "Vs": Agriculture May Have Shaped Both Human Jaws and Language by Anne Pycha (March 14, 2019)

Each author biography was accurate at the time the article was originally published.

INDEX

A

Africa, 36, 38, 80–81, 96, 109, 111–118, 132, 137, 141–142, 150, 153
atheism, 29, 57, 59

B

behavior, 78–79, 92, 94–96, 108, 143–145, 150–151
Bible, 24, 27, 30–31, 36, 38, 44–45, 50, 52–53, 59, 61, 63
bipedalism, 27, 113, 132–142
Branch, Glenn, 44–46, 52–54, 63–71
Buddhism, 64
Butler Act, 44–46, 53

C

Cambrian, 99
Carroll, Sean B., 14–22
Cenozoic, 103
Christianity, 17, 29, 31–32, 37, 50–51, 56–57, 64
climate change, 34, 41, 69–71
Cloutier, Richard, 120–131
Constitution (U.S.), 20, 63
courts, 6, 20, 45, 52–54, 66–67 *See also* Supreme Court (U.S.)
COVID-19, 15–16, 21–22, 36, 41, 83–85, 143
creationism/special creation, 8–10, 15–20, 23–24, 30–32, 36–38, 40, 44–61, 63, 65–68
Cretaceous, 30, 102–103

D

Darwin, Charles
  Darwinism, 17, 23–27
  Descent of Man, The, 108, 110
  humans, 108–112, 140
  On the Origin of Species, 10, 25, 91, 108, 120
  social Darwinism, 110
DeSilva, Jeremy, 132–142
Devonian, 121–123, 125, 128
dinosaur, 28, 30–31, 98, 100–102
DNA, 86–90, 96, 109, 116–118

E

Earth
  age of, 8–12, 24, 28, 30
  geology, 8–9, 11–12, 18, 28, 31
  origins of life, 86–90, 98
education
  academic freedom, 45, 52

avoidance, 50–52, 55, 57, 70
ban on evolution, 44–45, 52–53, 63, 66
laws, 6, 44–46, 52–54, 67, 69–71
standards, 63–64, 67–70
teachers, 37, 49–57, 63–71
teaching both sides, 36, 45, 47–48, 52, 67
teaching creationism, 32, 51–53, 60, 66
textbooks, 23, 38, 45, 46, 60, 64, 67
training, 40, 49, 51–52, 55–56, 59–60, 64
undermining religion, 17, 20
See also courts
evolution
denial of, 15–22
evidence of, 6, 10, 28–31, 44, 47, 49–51, 58
misconceptions, 54–56
sound, 98–106
theistic, 10, 47
Extance, Andy, 86–90
extinction, 6, 75–77, 84–85, 98, 112, 117, 140

F

First Amendment, 20, 63
fossil record, 12, 18, 30–31, 98–106, 108–109, 111–118, 121–152
Frayer, David W., 143–151

G

genetics, 25, 33, 36, 75–76, 79, 86–90, 96–97, 116–117, 120, 128, 130, 150
Galápagos Islands, 75–77, 96
Goldman, Jason G., 78–81, 96–97

H

Habib, Michael B., 98–106
HMS *Beagle*, 9, 110
hominid, 18, 28, 31
hominin, 109, 111–119, 132–142
Hopper, Allison, 36–39
humans
body, 120–142, 152–154
Denisovan, 77, 115–117
Homo erectus, 111, 113, 115–116, 136, 139
Homo floresiensis, 114–115, 140
Homo sapien, 108–109, 111–118, 132, 135, 152
Neanderthal, 77, 111, 115–118, 143–151
hybridization, 76–77, 117

I

Intagliata, Christopher, 73–74
Islam, 32, 56

J

Jehovah's Witness, 56
Judaism, 64
Jurassic, 30

K
Kane, Jonathan, 28–32
Keesey, T. Michael, 28–32

L
Landrum, Asheley R., 33–35
language, 105–106, 113, 116, 148–150, 152–154
Lawson, Lucinda, 75–77
Levin, Michael, 91–95
Long, John A., 120–131

M
Mesozoic, 100, 103
Miller, Kenneth, 23–27
Miocene, 141–142

N
Naish, Darren, 28–32
National Center for Science Education (NCSE), 40, 52–53, 55, 66–67
natural selection, 6, 8, 11–12, 19, 24–25, 33, 38, 55–56, 91–92, 108, 110
Neolithic, 152

O
Oreskes, Naomi, 21, 40–42

P
Paleolithic, 146, 152–153
Piore, Adam, 49–62
Pliocene, 134, 136, 141
politics, 30, 33–35, 46, 67, 69–71
Pycha, Anne, 152–154

R
racism, 24–25, 36–39, 110
Radovčić, Davorka, 143–151
Reid, Ann, 44–46, 66–68
religion, 6, 10, 17, 21, 23, 28, 33, 36, 45–47, 49–60, 64, 70, 83, *See also* atheism; Buddhism; Christianity; Islam; Jehovah's Witness; Judaism
RNA, 86–91

S
science
- bias in, 40–42
- denial of, 14–22, 33–39, 44–47
- trust in, 40–42, 53

Scopes, John T., 44, 53, 65–66
Singham, Mano, 8–13
Supreme Court (U.S.), 20, 46, 53–54, 63

T
Triassic, 147

U
Unitarianism, 64

W
Willoughby, Emily, 28–32
Wong, Kate, 108–119

Y
Yuste, Rafael, 91–95